PURPLE MONKEYS!

A Leader's Practical Guide To Unleashing The Power Of Questions To Achieve Great Results

Kevin Parker

Published by New Generation Publishing in 2013

Copyright © Kevin Parker 2013

First Edition

The author asserts the moral right under the Copyright, Designs and Patents Act 1988 to be identified as the author of this work.

All Rights reserved. No part of this publication may be reproduced, stored in a retrieval system or transmitted, in any form or by any means without the prior consent of the author, nor be otherwise circulated in any form of binding or cover other than that which it is published and without a similar condition being imposed on the subsequent purchaser.

www.newgeneration-publishing.com

New Generation Publishing

Acknowleagements

I am truly indebted to the many people who knowingly and sometimes unknowingly have been important in helping me complete this book. There are many colleagues and clients whose skills and knowledge have brushed off on me over the years.

In particular I would like to thank my close colleagues, John Bull, Lorraine Steele, Sarah Cartwright, Marianne O'Connor, Roger Lloyd-Thompson, Jill Morrow, Gilly Salter and Matt Driver for providing me with ideas, feedback and encouragement. Also to Maz White and Sophie Workman for supporting me at our office.

Valerie Simeoni and Stephen Friar provided wonderful support in correcting the many grammatical and syntax errors, and checking that what I had written seemed to at least to make some sense.

Thanks to all those who contributed examples of great questions they have come across – they are named later in the book.

I want to thank my son David and my daughter Bethan, for always being an inspiration and asking me 'why' when they were little, and more often why not when they grew older! Finally I would like to dedicate this book to my Mum and late Dad who always encouraged me to ask questions, never scolded me too much when I made mistakes, always listened to me and others, and who always supported me to be the best I could be.

Introduction

Most of us enter management because we were good at what we did. But promotion brings with it the formidable challenge of influencing others to achieve things, rather than doing them ourselves! This can be an unnerving prospect, one that some leaders struggle with all their careers. But there is a way to meet it: instead of trying to have all the answers, be good at asking great questions! It really is amazing how learning to ask a few powerful questions can transform an OK manager into a successful leader!

How can you expect to have all the answers today's complex, rapidly developing world? (Leave that to Google!)

In order to build high performing organisations we need to engage people more effectively and to harness their potential. Ask the right questions in the right way, and you will discover a powerful tool that can help people think through their own choices and make their own decisions, resulting in greater motivation and commitment.

So why Purple Monkeys? I often challenge participants on my programmes with: Don't think of purple monkeys for the next ten seconds. They of course can't. And that's part of the power of questions. They help the brain focus on what's in the question

If I ask: *Can you do this?* Rather than: *How can you do this?* You focus in two different ways. The first focuses you on whether something is possible to achieve. The second assumes it is possible, and focuses on how you go about making it happen.

When you learn to ask the right questions with the right 'purple monkey' you can provide focus, build awareness and responsibility, manage emotions, challenge assumptions, unleash creativity, accelerate learning and develop momentum,

I hope this book stimulates you and generates a lasting passion for asking challenging questions. It seeks to focus on this essential but under-utilised capability - the skill and art of asking powerful questions - and provides you with some really effective ones that you can add to your armoury.

It is my intention that as a result of reading this book you will become a more influential and effective leader. I have aimed to make it as user-friendly as possible: you can dip into it or read it from cover to cover and it's small enough to fit in your briefcase. I believe it will make a significant contribution to helping today's leaders meet tomorrow's challenges more successfully.

So ask yourself:

'How much better might I perform as a leader if were to ask better questions?'

and

'How good a question is that?'

During my leadership programmes, participants often ask for lists of good questions they can use. Consequently, many examples of great questions will be found in these pages, but I aim also to give insights into:

- How you ask powerful questions

- How to focus your questions for the best results

- How to develop a listening mind-set.

Introduction

Therefore, rather than simply providing lists of questions, the book is structured to enable you to consider the specific challenges that powerful questions will help you address at work, and why certain questions will work better in these situations than others.

> *You can tell whether a man is clever by his answers. You can tell whether a man is wise by his questions.*
>
> **Naguib Mahfouz**

This book will furnish you with some of the best questions that leaders ask. They are drawn from writers on the subject and directly from executives I meet and work with. My aim is to provide you with some great questions you can ask together with a more detailed explanation of how and why they work so well.

Firstly I spend some time looking at the difference between good questions and powerful questions and the principles you can adopt to make your questions more powerful

I have then grouped examples of great questions you can use facing different challenges, i.e. what are the situations you face in your daily work life and which questions you could draw on to help you. Each challenge is further subdivided into:

- An introduction – some context for this section

- The best questions to ask here – examples of great questions or great questions to ask and the rationale behind them

The next section includes examples of the best questions provided by named leaders from all walks of life categorised in terms of questions they have been:

- Asked,

- Been asked

- Wish they had asked,

These have been contributed directly by them, together with some of the context behind them. I have then added some comment. Others have been drawn from biographies and autobiographies (*see* Bibliography).

Of course if you ask lots of questions you have to be good at listening to the responses. In fact the better you are at listening the better you will find your questions are. The answer to a question is often, as my colleagues Sarah and Marianne say, the mother of the next question

This section is followed by a discussion on how you get started in asking better questions and how if you ask them you should be ready to respond to difficult questions asked of you

Finally I have pulled together a list of the best questions I have found drawn from all parts of the book. I hope you find them useful and start to adopt them as part of your working and, indeed, in your private life.

I am a passionate advocate of asking great questions and enjoy seeing people grow and take responsibility as they think through the answers. I am sure you will start to feel the same way.

This book is intended to live and grow and we would be delighted to have any feedback, suggestions and examples. If you do wish to make any comments or suggest questions you can do so easily at our website www.pmpgenesis.net

If you would like to join me via *twitter* or *linked in* I will be blogging and tweeting regularly on the subject

> *Before I refuse to take your questions, I have an opening statement.*
> **Ronald Reagan**

Contents

Why Not Skip This Bit? 1
What Makes a Powerful Question? 14
How Can Questions Provide Focus? 42
How Can Questions Manage Emotions? 59
How Can Questions Build Self-Awareness? 76
How Can Questions Challenge Assumptions? 86
How Can Questions Develop Momentum? 103
How Can Questions Unleash Creativity? 114
How Can Questions Accelerate Learning? 126
How Can Questions Increase Assertiveness? 134
How Can Questions Grow Responsibility? 155
What Could I Learn About Listening? 165
Real Examples From Leaders 182
How Can I Start? 191
In Conclusion 197
Appendix - The Best Powerful Questions List 199
About The Author 205
Bibliography 209

Why Not Skip This Bit?

The Leader

I wanna be the leader

I wanna be the leader

Can I be the leader?

Can I? I can?

Promise? Promise?

Yippee I'm the leader

I'm the leader

OK what shall we do?

Roger McGough

I first became aware of the real power of questions when my boss, the new CEO of the company where I had just become Head of Human Resources, asked me: 'How do you manage your department Kevin?' This floored me because I had never really thought about it. I was new to a management role, I had my team and we did our job. But how did we know what to do, what the company wanted, whether I was organised to meet the needs and ultimately how the hell did I know whether what I was doing was the right thing anyway (other than that I would soon know if I did something badly)? During the next few months he helped me think it through.

What I learned from this experience was that, surprisingly, he rarely gave me any advice! He simply asked questions that made me think, spurred me to action and as a result I developed a strong ownership and commitment to the outcome.

Why Not Skip This Bit?

I also learned that to be a great boss, you don't need to have the answers, you just need to ask great questions and listen to the answers. My boss is still memorable to me now for many things, but the questions he asked are the memories that stay in my mind more than anything else.

Many of us reach our first management or leadership position by being good technically at what we do. We are good accountants, or good marketers, or good engineers. When we get promoted to a management role for the first time we face an entirely different challenge. How do we engage and motivate others to do what we used to do? The temptation is to carry on trying to do things ourselves or at least tell others how to do it. This is unsustainable for a two key reasons:

- How can we have all the answers anyway? It's a complex fast changing world, and what do we really know?

- Once we become a leader, it's not our role to just supply answers any more. Even if we could, what would it do to the commitment and motivation of those who work for us?

So lets look at these points in turn

How can we have all the answers anyway? Change is almost the one constant in today's world. My son, David, is involved in marine conservation and my daughter Beth, an environmental geographer, is involved with cleaning water, using electricity - jobs that probably didn't exist ten years ago. I love my iPhone and find I use it for so many things. If you had asked me to imagine such a device 10 years ago I am certain I could not have done so.

> *True wisdom comes to each of us when we realise how little we understand about life, ourselves, and the world around us*
>
> **Socrates**

One of my historic heroes is the Greek Philosopher, Socrates - the grandfather of questions. Born in 470 BC he spent his life questioning the conventional wisdom of the day. So much so in fact that he was seen by the authorities of the time as disruptive and they accused him of corrupting the youth of the day. He was tried, found guilty and forced to take poison.

He realised early in his life not how much people knew, but how much **they didn't know**, by his use of questioning. He established the principle that everything is open to question and that there can be no cut and dried answers, because even these answers are open to further questioning.

This questioning did far more than expose the ignorance of the so-called wise, it stimulated great interest amongst all who saw him at his art. As people became excited and stimulated by seeing conventional wisdom being challenged they themselves became more self-aware.

It is doubtful whether any philosopher has been as influential as Socrates and this has been felt right down through the centuries until this day. He himself said he had no positive techniques to offer, only questions to ask.

His approach evolved into the Dialectic or Socratic method of teaching. This questioning approach is not applicable for the simple basic imparting of information but is best applied where there is an empathetic relationship between teacher and pupil. Here the teacher prompts the pupil step by step in the right direction by use of questions alone. You could say then that not only was he the grandfather of questions but also of coaching itself.

And so to more modern times. In the last 100 years profound changes have taken place in science and technology. I would say that two great conventional wisdom-shattering scientific upheavals in particular have occurred

Einstein's theory of relativity superseded much of traditional science. If this wasn't enough then along came Quantum theory.

Now both of these theories are seen to this day to be logically incompatible, and yet each of them produces results that are every bit as accurate as each other. How is it possible? Or is equally likely that both of them are wrong? Both of them are used every day by scientists and give extremely accurate results.

What does this say to us? Even the best of our knowledge is made up of man made theories about the world that may well be open to question. In fact we now fully expect most of them to be replaced as time goes by with some new breakthrough in thinking.

Our human knowledge is just that, human, and is therefore open to challenge and fallibility as we all are. Knowledge it seems is not as cast iron as we once believed.

If therefore, the scientific logical more provable world is open to challenge, then what of the very uncertain business world we live in?

Socrates was and still is right - if no knowledge is absolute then questioning is a powerful and essential process and approach to life. It is also of no surprise that the best practitioners in every field are interested in a healthy questioning approach to their area of expertise.

Did these people, do you think, ever ask themselves the right questions?

This 'telephone' has too many shortcomings to be seriously considered as a means of communication. The device is inherently of no value too us. - Western Union internal memo 1876

We don't like their sound, and guitar music is on the way out. - (Response to the music of 'The Beatles' in 1962) Decca Recording Company

Inventions have long since reached their limit, and I see no hope for further development. - Julius Sextus Frontinus (ca. 40–103 AD)

Louis Pasteur's theory of germs is ridiculous fiction. - Pierre Pachet

Everything that can be invented has been invented. (1899) - Commissioner of Patents

I think there is a world market for maybe five computers. - Thomas Watson IBM

To earn the right to compete and even just survive in this the 21st Century, organisations have to put aside the mindset of 'built to last' and look afresh at the challenges they face from the perspective of 'built to change'. The challenge facing any business leader today is how we create dynamic 'thinking' organisations – ones that have greater focus, commitment, innovation, engagement and action? In other words how do we build a capability in an organisation to continually deliver better performance than competitors? How do we develop a new style leadership that will deliver this?

> *'Leading from good to great does not mean coming up with the answers and motivating everyone to follow your messianic vision. It means having the humility to grasp the fact that you do not yet understand enough to have the answers, and then ask the questions that will lead to the best possible insights'*

From 'Good to Great' Jim Collins

I have, possibly like you, experienced working in old-fashioned autocratic organisations. These seem to assume that most people do their best when they are afraid, and that the leader somehow has all the

Why Not Skip This Bit?

answers. In today's complex fast moving world, we need more than ever to build responsibility right throughout the organisation. You can't do that by telling people what to do. You can only achieve this by getting people to think for themselves and take responsibility for what they do.

Let me give you a metaphor that illustrates this. How many of us always drive within the speed limit? I guess most of us would say we always try and drive safely. But when do we definitely drive within the speed limit - I suspects it's when we see a speed camera or policeman nearby. Some people will always drive within the speed limit for environmental or absolute safety reasons. They are committed to do so. Most of us are simply complying. In organisations where people are simply complying what do you need? You need the equivalent of policemen and speed cameras. Think about the amount of resource this takes. What would be the result if everyone were committed to the cause, rather than just complying with it?

The scope of skills that the modern leader needs is now much wider. On top of the traditional performance management and planning skills - leaders are expected to have a wide range of skills for thinking strategically and creatively, for influencing and engaging a growing number of stakeholders (many of whom are beyond their 'direct' control), and for executing ideas into action at almost impossible speeds.

The most effective style of leadership has become one known as 'achievement led' - where leaders set high standards, but then allow people to take a far more active role in thinking through and driving forward the best way to achieve these standards.

A great example of this is the British Cycling Team. Can you imagine these highly motivated performers even existing and far less performing, in an organisation where they were told what and how to do things? And yet this team is the most successful in history. (Even getting the French to believe they were using rounder wheels!)

As in today's complex world we as leaders cannot possibly have all the answers anyway, isn't the best approach therefore always to draw answers and ideas from others? The speed of technological innovation and other progress often leaves prescriptive managers lost for answers. Tell, instruct, command and control can only really work when the teller possesses more knowledge than the told.

Leaders who ask more questions are not solely dependent on their own knowledge and experience. They can access both the current and the latent capability of those they manage. This skill is becoming increasingly necessary in today's business climate. Recognising this is not weakness, but a rather it's a strength. While there is no one easy solution for tomorrow's leaders, this approach or change in mindset is needed.

Leadership from the top, while more important than ever is vital but not sufficient. Organisations have to develop their leadership capability at all levels and in all people. Today's leaders challenge is to help everyone reach his or her maximum potential.

The key to gaining commitment is allowing people to make the choice to do something rather than being forced to do it. We know from workplace studies that the biggest factor in employee satisfaction is the degree of control people have over their jobs, assuming other factors such as the pay and the hours are somewhere in the normal range. People like choice more than they like the thing they choose.

For example, suppose a magic genie gave you these two choices:

You can eat at the finest restaurants in the world for free, twice a week. The catches are that the genie picks the day, and he picks the specific restaurant.

Why Not Skip This Bit?

Or...

You can eat at 'good' restaurants, again for free, twice a week. But this time you can schedule it whenever you want, up to two places per week, and pick whatever 'good' restaurant you want.

Your first impulse might be to pick the finest restaurants in the world. I suspect you would eventually start to resent the genie's control over your life. You would become jaded about the fine dining experience, and you would never get used to the genie having so much control over your options.

If you took the 'good' restaurant option, and had full control of the when and where, you would fully enjoy it. If you wanted some fine dining, you could always pay for it yourself, and it would feel special.

The main point here is how many things make sense when viewed through this filter of choice-equals-happiness.

When you make your own choices, no matter what you choose, it seems like a better option than it really is because *you* chose it. I believe that, without even the benefit of seeing any research, a box of mixed chocolate tastes better than a non-mixed box purely because of the choice.

Here's a tip for you to try. It simply follows from the choice equals happiness idea we have looked at. The next time your friend or colleague is arguing with you over a decision, try and make it seem that it is their choice.

For example, let's say you favour Option A, and someone else wants Option B for reasons that seem to you irrational. You are at an impasse. Change the question to this:

'Do you want Option A with this risk, or do you want Option B with this other risk? It's your call.'

When you put things in the form of a choice, sometimes it gives people the only thing they wanted in the first place.

So what we are talking about here is adopting a different approach. It is definitely still leadership but using a new mindset – the leader as an engager, a facilitator, a coach, or someone who asks questions to help people think through what and why they are doing something, and then helps them make the choice for themselves.

My interest in questions started from an early age. When I reflect on earlier memories, the teachers I most remember in school are those who prompted me to think, rather than those who employed learning by rote. It was their questions that sparked my interest. I remember my geography teacher fondly. He once asked; 'Why, when you look at clouds in the sky, do they often appear in layers down to the horizon?' I was fascinated by this and found out. Clouds are often at the about same level, so what you are actually seeing is the curvature of the earth!

During my career as a management consultant I became skilled at facilitating workshops and came to realise that of all the skills I thought I had, the one my clients remarked about most often was that I asked good questions. I would never need to control a group by power of personality or brilliance of concepts (thank god or I would really have been in trouble!), but because I could ask a question in the middle of a heated often negative debate like 'What would you rather have?' and stop them in their tracks.

When I left my job as senior partner of a large consulting practice to start life as an independent consultant, I participated in a course that changed my life and brought to absolute clarity the power of questions. The course was NLP (Neuro Linguistic Programming) and I soon followed up this new-found awareness and thirst for knowledge by training to be a coach.

Why Not Skip This Bit?

In my work as a coach I see the power of questions every day. I enjoy seeing the effect of often simple but powerful questions stopping people in their tracks and making them think. The other day when coaching a CEO in a new role in a new organisation where he was struggling to make an impact, I asked ' So what did you have in place around you when you were successful before?' Within minutes he was pouring out masses of positive ideas and had lost his negativity. Why it is we are not able to ask these questions of ourselves I have never been sure but I guess its something to do with perspective and that's why, luckily for me, people buy coaching and consulting

So what kind of questions are we talking about here? I am talking about the kind of questions that make people think and that can build their awareness and help them take responsibility. As leaders and managers, our role is not simply to ask questions, which enable us to make better decisions for everyone else. We want everyone in our organisations to fulfil their own potential, become self-motivated and make the decisions for themselves. To do this we have to get people to think more for themselves. The right questions, or as I have named them 'Powerful Questions', are the vehicles for achieving just this.

In order to respond to these challenges I strongly advocate tomorrow's leaders adopting a more coaching style, wonderfully explained in I think in John Whitmore's classic book 'Performance Coaching'. My aim in this book is slightly different. It is quite a big commitment for today's managers to become a coach. **It is though, a much smaller step to become better at one aspect of coaching – that of asking powerful questions.**

This book **is** about recognising what a huge difference everyone can make simply by asking more and better questions. It is about encouraging people to ask more and better questions, especially those that make people stop and think and then act differently. Much of my consulting success has come from asking the great questions no one else is prepared to ask.

Let's look at in more detail at some of the benefits of asking powerful questions.

Asking powerful questions demonstrates first that you're listening (and if you ask a powerful question you'll be interested in the answer which helps to focus your listening more!), and this always helps to build and strengthen relationships. Think of a conversation recently when someone asked very few or maybe didn't ask you even a single question. How did you feel about that? How did you feel about that person? How interested would you be in talking to him or her in the future? By starting to ask more questions in all of your discussions, you'll find you gain powerful information to improve your own performance, strengthen relationships, and reduce mis-understandings.

Asking good questions is they key element of any conversation that encourages us to suspend our assumptions and as a result better understand another person's point of view. Assumptions often lead to miscommunications, mismatched expectations, stress, damaged relationships or tasks not completed. The simple act of clarifying and confirming what you understand to be true, and seeing if others have a similar understanding, can get rid of the downside of making too many assumptions.

To help you to do this, ask questions that ensure you have a common understanding of what is being discussed, and what action needs to be taken. For example, the seemingly obvious question, 'How will you be making sure that happens?' would ensure that one person is taking responsibility for an action item, and no two people are doing the same task.

> *Asking the right questions takes as much skill as giving the right answers.*
>
> **Robert Half**

Any unasked (and thus, unanswered) question is a trap door waiting to open under your feet. Think about a team whose members put forward their ideas, but don't take the time to understand colleagues' ideas or bring discussions to closure. The length and frequency of their meetings can soar, while actual progress creeps along at a snail's pace. By taking time to ask thoughtful questions of each person, you demonstrate your respect for each person and his ideas, which boosts morale and can increase employees' contributions to the business.

When people have the information that they need to do their jobs best, the organisation benefits from increased productivity and individuals reap the rewards of high morale and low stress (both are products of having - rather than hoarding - information). How do people get the information they need? By asking. First of all, most people can't read others' minds. So, the information won't come if not solicited. Secondly, it is the individual's responsibility to ask for what's needed - no one else should manage this.

Complex problems have complex solutions and these solutions rarely exist at the level the problem is observed. Searching to find what lies underneath is the route to sustainable success. How would you feel if your doctor prescribed before diagnosing what was wrong? (*Doctor: I've organised your heart transplant. Patient: But I only have a headache!*). If someone is not working or doing something effectively, telling them to 'buck up' is unlikely to make much of a difference. There is usually some underlying problem maybe about competence, motivation or lack of awareness that is the cause. You are unlikely to find that reason by guessing.

As a management team you might be managing an area of underperformance. You take action A but results continue to deteriorate. You take action B but results continue to deteriorate. You take action C but results continue to deteriorate. You take action D and results improve significantly. Which action delivered the improvement? The lazy management often will choose action D. Better leaders ask questions to really understand what happened, what can be learned and what can be drawn from this to help in the future. Poor managers who don't ask the right questions are doomed to repeat their failures.

Questions we ask people stimulate their thinking processes. When you stimulate their thinking processes, you give them the chance to express their own ideas and feelings. The only way you will find out what you want to know about another is by asking questions. If you are able to help people think on their own they will respect you and like you. You have been able to do something for them that they were not able to do for themselves. By listening to others, you also fulfil their need to feel valued. Through your concern, they feel special.

No one ever listened themselves out of a job.

Calvin Coolidge, Past US President

What Makes a Powerful Question?

The true voyage of discovery lies not in seeking new landscapes,

But in having new eyes.

Marcel Proust

Questions focus another person's attention in a way that a statement or presentation would find much harder to achieve. Why, because this is the way the brain works. At the end of the day people make decisions and take actions based on their own logical and intuitive reasoning. A presentation or statement **may** engage someone's thinking, while a question will **always** do this.

Consider this question: What's the weather like right now?

Even though it's a pretty routine question I suspect your mind went straight away to consider it. So even though you knew you were unlikely to have to furnish me with an answer you still did this. We love answering questions. Quiz shows are some of the most popular shows on television and many of the most successful board games like 'Trivial Pursuits' are about questions.

But I am not talking here about simple questions or ones that test your general knowledge. I'm talking about questions that challenge your thinking, that get you to think about something differently, that increase your self-awareness or that build your responsibility.

From the time we were small children, we've been taught to pursue the right answer. Our parents asked us to correctly identify pictures in a book. Teachers gave us tests to check our understanding of a subject. We interviewed for jobs hoping to answer the interviewer's questions correctly. And at work we are constantly being asked to solve problems. Even in our leisure, we play games and watch TV game shows that challenge our ability to answer questions.

It's really quite amazing how much value we place on answers, considering an answer is only as good as the question that spurred it. An answer's value comes from its ability to solve a problem. A useful answer is more likely if the problem is properly defined, and a well-defined problem is usually stated in the form of a question.

More value lies in the question than in the answer.

To understand your effectiveness, begin evaluating the quality of the questions you ask. Successful people not only ask a lot of questions, they learn to ask powerful questions and then be very good listeners too.

What would happen then if I were to ask you a very incisive question, one that would really make you think about something?

(I'll pause a moment while you have to think about this)

The most effective leaders are inevitably the ones that ask the best questions. The way you ask questions and the types of questions you ask will determine the responses you get. By asking more and better questions you could add a very powerful tool to your armoury.

The way in which we ask a question sets the direction for the conversation.

The intent of a powerful question is:

- **Not for you to get information** so that you can make better decisions.

- **To help others reveal more**, to learn more, to open us up to see new possibilities and new solutions.

What Makes A Powerful Question?

Thus powerful questions lead to greater creativity.

Like many paradoxes of leadership, powerful questions gain their power from their simplicity. A powerful question is usually short and seemingly even 'dumb.' For example, 'What outcome do you want?' or 'What's the next step?' or 'What did you learn?' appear simple on the surface. But these questions cause people to become introspective and more reflective; thus, they are able to get to the heart of the matter.

Notice that powerful questions are often open-ended and 'what' questions. They move a conversation forward because they require reflection and more than a 'yes' or 'no' answer. Their intent is to go beyond getting information - it's to provide focus and to help us gain both insight and clarity.

Many of my clients come to me for coaching because they are looking for greater fulfilment at work, and one of the first questions I usually ask them is 'What would being fulfilled look like to you?'

When they get to the point where they can give me a fairly complete description, I then might ask; 'What do you need to do to make that happen?' And then we begin creating the steps they must take. The strength of this type of inquiry comes from its ability to elicit more personal authentic responses and to get people to think in a way that leads them to action.

Powerful questions also support collaboration because they enable everyone involved in the conversation to learn. They are great tools to use with teams in problem-solving. They make people stop and think. Because they arise from true curiosity, powerful questions are non-judgemental. There is no right or wrong answer. A simple question such as; 'What would that get us?' frees people to contemplate the possibilities. If this type of inquiry were used more often, it would help to shift beliefs. I find it hard to see, as an outsider anyway, how a company like HMV carried on with its retail outlets given the huge expansion of online music. Was anyone asking the right questions there?

Questions can be one of the most effective communication tools available to us. Strong relationships, strategic plans, award-winning collateral, and meaningful exchange of ideas and information are all products of asking skilful questions. If they're not, your communications could be weak or worthless, and you may experience miscommunications more often than necessary.

Why is the ability to ask skilful questions so powerful? Questions are the means we use to unearth new information, to compare our perspective with reality, and to learn more about what others are thinking and perceiving. When we don't ask questions, we're assuming that we know everything there is to know about the subject or the person. Is this ever the case? Rarely.

> Seek first to understand, and then to be understood
>
> **Dr Stephen Covey**

The Structure Of Powerful Questions

So successful people not only ask a lot of questions, they learn to ask *powerful* questions. But what does a powerful question look like? I have grouped powerful questions in the rest of the book under the benefits they achieve.

A powerful question challenges assumptions. Take the question, 'How do we improve morale?' This question assumes morale needs to be improved and that it can be improved. A better question might be 'How do we know if morale needs improving?'

What Makes A Powerful Question?

A diagram shows a central "?" surrounded by eight circles labeled: PROVIDE FOCUS, CHALLENGE ASSUMPTIONS, UNLEASH CREATIVITY, ACCELERATE LEARNING, GROW RESPONSIBILITY, INCREASE ASSERTIVENESS, DEVELOP MOMENTUM, BUILD AWARENESS, MANAGE EMOTIONS.

A powerful question pushes you to look at a problem from a new perspective. Take a simple question such as, 'What are the problems with our products?' Looking at the problem from another perspective, the question could be 'What aspects of our products do our customers admire?'

A powerful question encourages creativity. Imagine being part of a group trying to answer the question, 'What should we do for this year's holiday party?' Perhaps you'd rather be in the group working on the question, 'What can we do at the holiday party that will create a permanent, positive memory for the guests?'

A powerful question focuses. People struggle with global questions such as 'How do we improve quality?' A better question might be, 'In what ways can we use performance statistics to improve hold-times in our customer call centre?' When it comes to questions, it's critical to remember that you'll get what you ask for. Successful people are clear about what they want and ask powerful questions to move them quickly towards their goals.

A powerful question builds self-awareness. People are often unaware of their impact on others or how their view of a situation may be limiting their confidence. Telling someone they might have caused offence or antagonism by their actions or words is not an easy thing to do and often causes defensiveness or argument. Often asking the simple question 'How would you feel if you were the other person?' has a remarkable effect. This is often called transposing and the key thing is that once you have become aware of how someone else might be reacting it becomes virtually impossible for this not to affect your actions

A powerful question catalyses action. We all feel blocked from time to time and this traps us into inaction. Imagine for example asking someone 'What might you do if you knew you couldn't fail?' Getting people to move out of their blocked state if only for a few minutes opens up new possibilities – some of which are likely to be productive and stimulate action.

A powerful question helps learning. Everyone makes mistakes but we don't always learn from them. This is often because we feel a failure or feel guilty. There is also a tendency not to learn from success too. Asking, 'What could we do better next time?' for example focuses on the future and the positive

Leaders can't have all the answers. Although knowledge and wisdom are crucial, one person can't know everything. Wise leaders are curious. They realise that rather than having all the right answers it's more important to ask the right questions. Skilled leaders frame their questions to elicit as much learning as possible, and then they listen on several levels to the responses they are given.

How Can You Make Questions More Powerful?

It is not how smart you are:

But how you are smart

Howard Gardner

So what makes the difference between the levels of power of the questions you ask? The first thing to remember is what the intent of this type of question is in the first place. The aim is to:

- Make the other person or persons think

- Make them more aware

- Help them understand the choices they could make

The questions are **not** to show how clever *we* are!!

In this respect then we are aiming to establish a rapport, to make the other person feel we are genuinely interested in them and to show we have been listening. If we can help someone become less defensive and more receptive we have achieved our goal. Creating a feeling of safety and not one where people are feeling judged or interrogated is far more likely to achieve the results you want

Questioning can be a mark of respect for those you question. But only if you are focusing on *them* - thinking about how to draw out *their* views and sharpen *their* thoughts. In many cases, leaders find their attention drawn to the decision at hand, and so they blast a series of questions that may help them clarify their own thinking. When you are caught up in your own analysis, you can easily ignore the people side of your work - focusing on the 'hard' aspects of the decision and possible outcomes from it instead.

To avoid this question trap it may be wise to jot down your personal ideas and questions in a notebook as you talk - but not voice them right away. Instead, you might play the friendly reporter role in the conversation: Simply draw out a detailed, thoughtful presentation from the person you are listening to. Use your questions to probe *their* ideas and feelings, not your own. That is the mark of respectful listening: an obvious, active interest in what the other person's views are, not in developing your own.

OK, OK - you're in a hurry and you want to make a good decision quickly. And you think your people should be respectful of you as well. Fine! But think about this: Who is more likely to give you an open, fair hearing when it comes time to present your views: someone to whom you have listened with full respect and interest, or someone you have cross-examined as if they are just there to brief you, the great decision-maker, and then be led back to their desk?

So given all this how do you go about adding to the power of the questions you ask. From my experience, from talking to colleagues in the field and from the research carried out for this book a number of principles seem to emerge, which if you follow and get used to will help you add power to your questions.

I have grouped them into three types:

- Changing the words we use in our questions – in other words the **language** we use

- Changing the **scope** of the questions we use from narrow to wide, from small chunks to big chunks etc.

How Can You Make Questions More Powerful?

- Changing the intent of the questions we ask to get to what's under the surface – the **depth**.

I have called this the **L S D** architecture of powerful questions –

L anguage

S cope

D epth

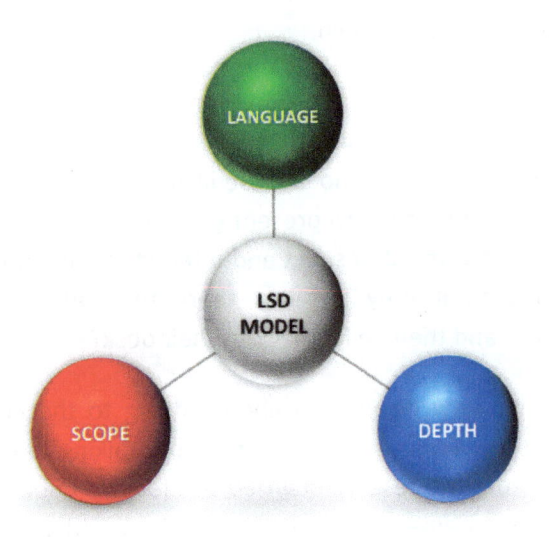

So let's have a look at these principles in more detail.

Changing the words we use in our questions – in other words the language we use

Principle #1   Use open not closed questions

This is on obvious one but easily forgotten. Open questions are called open because they open up the conversation and require more than a yes or no answer. Closed questions are closed because they do just that – they require a yes or no answer. The only times I have observed this not to be the case is when for example a TV interviewer is interviewing a politician. They refuse to answer closed questions with a yes or no.

Q: Is it true that your opposition to building a new rail link will cause global warming?

A: It is not as simple as that ...

So for example 'Are you feeling ok today?' is a closed question and 'How are you feeling today?' is an open one

The only example I have where asking open questions elicits closed answers is when I used to talk to my teenage kids after school

Q: What did you do in school today?

A: Dunno

I am not saying that asking closed questions is wrong. Indeed there are times when it is important to bring a discussion to a conclusion or decision. But if you want someone to think more about a subject then ask more open questions. You might like to notice for a day your use of questions, and how often you ask open or closed ones. What would happen if you choose for a day to focus on asking more open questions to see what happens?

I have found that although everyone implicitly understands this difference, when it comes to application, they are often astounded when observers point out to them how many closed questions they ask, and as a result how difficult it was for the other person to become engaged in the conversation.

Closed questions often look like this and often begin with a verb:

How Can You Make Questions More Powerful?

Would you like vanilla ice cream?

Have you ever met Joan before?

So you've never been there before?

Are you happy?

Do you enjoy your car?

Does your brother have the same interests as you?

Do you have a pet?

Do you like animals?

Do you like rain?

Now, here are some examples of these close-ended questions turned into open-ended questions - to keep the conversation going. You will notice that none of them starts with a verb, instead they normally use what or how:

What is your favourite flavour of ice cream and why?

How did you meet Joan?

What do you feel was most beneficial about your school experience?

How can your top qualities help our organisation?

What are some of the things that bring you the most joy?

What made you decide to purchase a Seat?

What interests do you and your brother share, and which interests do you not share?

Do you have a pet and what is it like?

Do you like animals and what is it you like about them?

When is your birthday and how do you like to celebrate?

What is it you like about rain?

From these examples, it is clear that close-ended questions are used to elicit a short, quick response, while open-ended questions are gateways into conversations.

The best time to use closed questions is when you are summarising and clarifying. Here you might ask: 'So what we have agreed is that the way we have been asking questions up until now needs to change and that the best way forward is to buy lots of copies of this book? To which the answer of course is a simple 'yes'.

Principle #2   Use more of 'What' and 'Who' rather than 'When' and 'Where'. Avoid using 'Why'

Let's start with easy one - not using why. What makes me say that? (See you can avoid using why!) Well why questions tend to make people defensive. People feel in responding to a why question that they have to justify what they have done on a personal level. You might think what's wrong with that. Nothing if you want to interrogate someone and get them to admit their guilt. This might make you feel you have accomplished something but it has done little other than promote a very guilty feeling in the other person, and a reluctance in them 'not to go there again'. If you want someone to open up and think more positively about things then we have to try a different approach.

Consider for a moment how these two questions feel to you.

- Why did you do that?

- What caused that to happen?

The second tends to depersonalise and help the person being questioned to talk about the subject in a more relaxed way.

When I hear leaders ask people 'why' on a regular basis, or extoll the virtues of the '5 whys,' I cringe. 'Why' is a great question for research, but when we really want to fix interpersonal and work issues, it's actually a problem.

For example consider how you might respond if I were to ask you: 'Why haven't you completed this project?' Or, 'Why didn't you do that business analysis two months ago when I asked?

I bet many of you were guiltily transported back to a time in your life when a question like that was asked and how it made you feel. Not too great I expect

Now, instead, what if I asked you: 'What's getting in the way of finishing this, and what would need to happen to deliver it by the end of next week?'

The 'why' question asks you to justify or explain to me the unchangeable past which is not that helpful anyway. Whereas the 'what' question helps you sharpen your focus pragmatically on outcome.

'What' questions will get you an understanding of the structure of a problem. 'Why' questions are likely to get you justifications and reasons without changing anything.

Now I'm going to ask you to try an experiment. What would happen if you were to ban 'why' questions for a period of time? Try this for say two weeks and describe what you notice. Also notice how people react when others ask them 'why.'

My own experience is very positive using this approach. I've found it a valuable tool over many years.

When learning and getting to the root of issues so that the problem can be solved is your goal, I suggest you focus on results-oriented questions such as what and how. They will enable you to increase effectiveness and be a great model for others.

So now let's move on to when and where. These are definitely not as 'hard' as why questions and do have their role when you want someone to be more specific. However they are best used later in a discussion rather that the first question you ask because that very specific-ness they promote can feel a bit threatening at first.

Undoubtedly the best word to start a question is 'what'. It usually promotes objectivity and not defensiveness. Initially might find it clumsy to start using 'what' at the beginning of a question instead of 'why', 'when' and 'where', but with practice you will find the benefits you get from the answers you receive are well worth it.

Here are some examples:

Why Question	Using A What Question Instead
Why did you do that?	What led you to do that?
Why did that happen?	What caused that to happen?
Why are you doing that?	What's behind you doing this?
Why have you not done that yet?	What's stopping you from doing that?
Why did you ask me that?	What made you ask me that?

Principle #3   Use conditional (could, might etc.) and future tenses

When we ask questions about the past it can seem rather like asking 'why' questions - a bit personal and can this make people defensive or make them feel not so good about themselves. Now I know this will not always be the case and sometimes it is useful to examine the past, but what I am suggesting is that you focus on the future first. The future has not happened yet, and that is where we will be spending our lives. It is an area of freedom and possibilities, where we can potentially still learn from the past, but not be trapped by it. I would even suggest trying to stay out of the present too for similar, but not so compelling, reasons.

So for example rather that interrogate someone about what happened and why they did something, ask:

'In what ways can you make things better in the future?'

Another way to use the future, so to speak, is to use questions to take us there and look back. Sometimes you can get an entirely different perspective by asking something like:

Imagine we have achieved our sales goal in a year's time, what would we have to have done to achieve it?

Similarly to keep someone in the open mode and not weighed down by the past or obligations, using the conditional tense adds greatly to the power of your question. Consider for a moment the difference between

What are you going to do about it?

And

What might you do about it?

The first question has a feeling of obligation or even command about it. Whenever someone feels they are responding to what they might feel is a demand, there is a likelihood that they become defensive. If they become defensive you have of course lost the power of the question.

So for lets look at changing a simple question like: 'Will you buy me a drink?' to 'Could you please buy me a drink?' The second version is more like asking if the person you are speaking to has the ability to buy you a drink. Does he have time to do it, does he have any change to pay for it, etc. It feels far less challenging

Using the conditional tense with such words as 'might' or 'could' (but not 'ought' for reasons you should be able to guess by now) will make a real difference to the way people respond to your questions.

Usual Question	Using The Conditional Approach
When are you going to do this?	When could you do this?
How are you going to do this?	How might you do this?
What ideas have you got?	What ideas might you have?
What problems will you encounter?	What problems could you encounter?
How will you overcome them?	How might you overcome them?

Principle #4   Keep the question as short and uncluttered as possible.

You want the receiver to focus on the answer, not understanding the question. Research has shown that we focus far more on the beginning and the end of words, sentences, stories, and presentations. If you make you question too long the recipient will miss most of it anyway.

How Can You Make Questions More Powerful?

Try and read the paragraph below:

Dufficilt qeunstios ofefr us a unuiqe optporutniy to gian gatreer inshigt itno the key croncens of our aundiece. The key to wininng oevr a dlificuft poesrn is to resecpt and acnogkwlede tiher cencorn as haivng a pisitove intention from tehir pinot of view.

I suspect you were able to, reasonably easily, and this emphasises the point.

In particular it is easier to ask shorter questions when you have been listening well. For example someone tells you that something has caused them a problem and you respond 'In what way?' - simple but powerful!

Try and shorten these questions (possible answers at the end of the chapter)

- What different ways are you considering going about this plan of action?

- What are the reasons behind this decision to go ahead with this plan?

- At what times do feel more confident or less confident to deal with the situation you have explained?

I remember reading a story about a writer who had written books about how to achieve your goals in life etc. He was being interviewed on the radio and also had listeners call in. One listener was quite angry and said something to the effect that it was all right for middle class educated people to talk about goals and dreams. He was working hard just to survive. The writer listened and responded by asking ' If you could have a goal what would it be'. The listener paused and said; I've always wanted to be a mechanic but I have none of the skills.' The writer replied; 'Yet'. The listener simply ended the phone call. A while later this writer reported that he had received a business card through the post in an envelope. It was the business card of that listener who was now a mechanic. Slightly puzzled just to have a business card he rang him to congratulate him and ask why he had just sent the card. The guy replied; 'Because I'm not very good at writing'. To which the writer replied; 'Yet!'

Sometimes simple single words stated in question form can be very powerful, such as:

'So..?'

'And …?'

Keeping questions short makes them more powerful because there is less distraction for the person on the receiving end, and they are more likely to open up in ways you might not have expected. Longer questions tend to distract and lead people more in a certain direction.

> I always like the story about a famous scientist and philosopher Blaise Pascal who wrote a long letter to a friend and apologised saying he was sorry he didn't have enough time to write anything shorter

Changing the scope of the questions we use from narrow to wide, from small chunks to big chunks etc.

Principle #5   Chunking Up or Down

Chunking up or down allows us to use questions to reach for higher meanings or search for more specific bits of missing information.

When we 'Chunk Up' the language gets more abstract and there are more chances for agreement, and when we 'Chunk Down' we tend to be looking for the specific details that may have been missing in the chunk up.

How Can You Make Questions More Powerful?

As an example if you ask the question; 'What is the purpose of cars?' You may get the answer; 'transport', which is a higher chunk and more towards the abstract.

If you asked; 'What do you like specifically about cars?' You will start to get smaller pieces of information about cars.

So when you are in an argument you might want to chunk up to find a level at which you agree. You might be arguing about children's' education and which ways are best. The argument is getting very heated and starting to boil over. You could ask a 'chunk up' question like; 'Can I check whether we all agree that everyone should have the same opportunity in education?' This would tend to help parties understand they were arguing about how and not what.

On the other hand you may be discussing how to downsize the organisation. Someone might be saying in general terms that the vulnerable need to be treated carefully. Ask a 'chunk down' question such as; 'Could you give me an example of what you mean by that?' This will clarify thinking and understanding

Principle #6   Adding More

Change from you to we, we to the organisation, one customer to all customers etc. This helps the receiver see the bigger picture. If someone is unable to see why they should be doing something then asking them something like; 'How does what your doing help the organisation?' might make them see it.

Simply changing from you to us in a question suggests to the receiver that he or she is not alone in the issue. For example think of the difference between these two questions:

How might you solve this problem?

And

How could we solve this problem?

Even though you want them to solve it for themselves, asking the question with 'we' in it is likely to elicit a more open response.

Principle #7   Change the perspective.

What would the situation look like from another point of view? This can be very powerful. Ask someone to see something from another point of view such as that of a colleague, a customer, a supplier or even a fictitious character (as we will see under the section on creativity).

I well remember the Executive team of a small technology company who were feeling stuck in terms of the next step in marketing their product. I asked them 'So, which entrepreneurs do you admire?' They answered Richard Branson. So I then asked; 'So what would Richard Branson do if he were faced with this problem?' They immediately came up with several ideas and indeed took one forward that was successful.

Changing someone's perspective can also be very powerful in building empathy where there is conflict between different people or groups. Empathy is a very powerful thing. The moment you feel empathy for someone else or for someone else's situation, it is unlikely you can stay mad with them for long.

So, asking

How might the other person be feeling about what you have said?

How would you feel if you were in their position?

Are great ways of changing perspective and building empathy.

Changing the intent of the questions we ask to get to what's under the surface - <u>the depth</u>

Principle #8   Challenge assumptions

Very often the problem we see on the surface is not the one that, when solved, will resolve the issue – there is often a deeper held belief or assumption or link that is causing the blockage.

Consider what assumptions the other person may be holding implicitly. They may say for example that they lack the resources to do something. Underneath may be a limiting assumption about whether this task is 'do-able' at all. So a way of getting to that assumption might be to challenge them in the question, 'What might we do if we had all the resources we needed?'

I have always been astonished how often this question breaks through limiting assumptions. In answering it, they come up with a lot of ideas which they realise they probably should be doing anyway.

So look out for assumptions people are making either explicitly or implicitly and use questions to challenge those assumptions rather than argue. So for example when someone says:

That will never work here

Try asking

What had led you to that conclusion?

Or

What would need to change to make it work here?

Whenever you hear anyone saying they must do something or they ought to do something then there is likely to be a built in assumption about some consequences if they don't do it. So when you here someone say: 'I ought to do this', then respond with: 'What would happen if you didn't?' and notice the response. It draws out their assumptions and hopefully they will end up saying the much more positive: 'I want to do this'. There is also much more chance of it happening

Principle #9   Look for cause and effect relationships

Challenge unclear or missing links, e.g. 'In what way does A cause B?' I must admit I would love to have the opportunity to ask questions of politicians on a news programme. If I did, this would be the type of question that I would use most often. The politicians will confidently state their case saying the reason why they are doing something and this link is left unchallenged. Asking them to explain the link in their thinking and justify it would on many occasions I think dismantle their argument.

Of course I am not suggesting that you use this type of question to destroy someone else's argument. What I am suggesting is that the reason someone may be blocked is because they are making an implicit link in their internal logic that may be false. Helping them to uncover the hidden link may well open them up completely to change, action and new ideas.

For example again when someone says

'We have tried that idea before and it won't work here.'

Your question might be

'So what caused it to fail last time?'

This uncovers the link. When you get the reply to this you can follow it up with,

'So does it always need to happen this way?'

You can imagine the rest.

Principle #10   Check for values and strongly held beliefs

This can be important in a number of ways. First of all an understanding of someone's values and beliefs will help you then work with that person. Secondly though getting to know someone's beliefs helps you, and them, understand what they value as important and interesting in life. Now we all feel motivated when we are doing things that interest us or we feel are important. So if you can find a way to link the task, project, etc. to their values, you might increase their motivation.

For example when discussing a task or job ask, 'What would that give you?' and 'What's important to you about this?' or 'What would make this task really motivating for you?'

I have put all these principles together in a diagram (below), which I have called the 'Power Web'. Now I'm not suggesting before you ask any question you stop yourself and look at this diagram to change your question. What I am suggesting is that you practice on worked examples, and also build your awareness by reflecting later on past conversations, to identify what worked and what didn't work.

A Worked Example

Will you finish the project on time?

Applying Principle #1 – Use Open Questions	Using Language 'Principles' to Add Power
When will you finish the project?	
Applying Principle #2 – Using What and How	
What do you need to complete the project on time?	
Applying Principle #3 – Using Conditional Tense	
What might you need to complete the project on time?	
Applying Principle #4 – Shorten the sentence	
What might you need for project success?	

Applying Principle #5 – Chunking up or down	Using Scope 'Principles' to Add Power
How might success with this project support our strategy?	
Applying Principle #6 – Adding more	
How could others support the success of this project?	
Applying Principle #7 – Changing perspective	
How could we delight the customer with this project?	

How Can You Make Questions More Powerful?

Applying Principle #8 – Challenging assumptions	Using Deeper Meaning 'Principles' to Add Power
What might we achieve if we had all the resources needed?	
Applying Principle #9 – Cause and effect	
What factors might have contributed to success here?	
Applying Principle #10 – Values and beliefs	
What could success here give you?	

So try this exercise for yourself on the following examples

- Why are you late so often?
- Why aren't you cooperating on this project?
- Why are our customers unhappy with our service?

Powerful Questions For You To Choose

The following chapters provide examples of questions and sets of questions you can use to address the areas shown in the diagram below.

```
              PROVIDE FOCUS
      MANAGE                CHALLENGE
     EMOTIONS              ASSUMPTIONS

  BUILD                          UNLEASH
AWARENESS         ?            CREATIVITY

   DEVELOP                       ACCELERATE
  MOMENTUM                        LEARNING

         INCREASE      GROW
       ASSERTIVENESS RESPONSIBILITY
```

You will be able to see how these 'Architecture Principles' are used in practice and be able to understand how you could add power to them in different situations.

Rather than simply provide lists of questions you could use for these challenges, I have provided some background and insights into this area so that you can see what some questions will work better than others

A Few Words Of Warning!

These questions are powerful and like a powerful car they need to be used carefully and with skill. Suddenly starting to use some of these questions when you have not been known to use them before might come as a shock to the recipient and they may wonder what has happened to you

Firstly remember your aim is to stimulate awareness and responsibility in others and you won't do this by making them become defensive or suspicious. Success inevitably comes from building rapport and this requires empathy and listening, as well as asking questions. I don't see a real contradiction here. If you really listen and have empathy with the other person then you will be curious and this curiosity will drive your questioning. By letting this happen you are in turn showing you are indeed listening and thus you build rapport.

Secondly think about softening the way you ask a question. For example rather than say 'What is your outcome here?' - you could soften it by saying 'I was wondering, listening to you, what success would look like'

Thirdly focus initially on the future not the past. Focusing on the past could bring up negative feelings, while focussing on the future is talking about things that have not happened yet and therefore there is little emotion or defensiveness attached.

Curiosity is one of the most permanent and certain characteristics of a vigorous mind.

Samuel Johnson

So what have we learned in this Chapter?

- The real difference between ordinary and powerful questions is?

- In what way do powerful questions add value?

- The principles for increasing the power of questions are?

- Why are we asking them?

How Can Questions Provide Focus?

'You've got to accentuate the positive. Eliminate the negative and latch on to the affirmative. Don't mess with Mister In-Between'

Words and Music by Harold Arlen and Johnny Mercer

Introduction

What is absolutely clear is that if we don't know what we are trying to achieve, we will have little chance of achieving it. And yet many of us go into situations without having a well thought through achievable outcome in our mind.

A while ago I was locked into a difficult situation. I desperately needed some information in order to conclude a business transfer that was important to the client and to the other associates working with me on the project. I chased and chased by phone, email and text with minimal response and progress. I was becoming more and more angry and frustrated and this was obviously leaking into the language of the messages I left. I was feeling in the right and he was in the wrong, but I was getting nowhere. I stopped and considered what I was doing. What I needed was the information and particularly his cooperation. It had to be a win-win too. I realised my aggressive approach would not get me the co-operation very easily.

So having thought about the outcome I wanted, I emailed apologising for the tone of the message, which might have seemed aggressive, and stating I knew we wanted the same thing. Two hours later he rang me and thanked me for the email and apologised for his slowness in response which was caused by factors beyond his easy control and which he was slightly embarrassed about. In a constructive conversation following this we sorted things out. Just reassessing the outcome made a huge change in my behaviour and the chances of success.

This chapter looks at the whole subject of outcome thinking and how it is such a vital pillar of leadership in general. It looks at:

- What makes a powerful outcome?
- How powerful outcomes change responses?
- How to ask questions that lead to powerful shared outcomes.

How many of us achieve everything in life we set out to do? If your answer to this is 'always' then email me your details - you have found the secret to success and we could start a new business venture. Most of us achieve far less than this - the average response I get when I ask this question on programmes I'm running is around 50% to 60%. But the key fact is that we all do achieve some of our goals, what we need to explore is what is going on when we succeed and what is going on when we don't.

So what's your focus in your life right now? Is it the goals and opportunities you have, or is it the multitude of problems that fill your life? Where you direct your thinking and approach have a huge impact on your success or otherwise.

Time and time again research has shown that people in all walks of life who focus on what they want, rather than the problems they have, achieve far greater success. They focus their energy on how to get around problems to achieve their outcome and they don't bother with issues that don't appear to be obstacles

This mode of thinking is often referred to as 'outcome thinking' or being 'goal-directed'. High performers tend to think naturally in an outcome or goal-directed way. Outcome thinking is one of the most powerful organising processes you can learn. It is a process of asking internal or external questions that direct our (or another's) mind, attention, and energy from a set of obstacles to a set of choices.

For example, if you ask, 'What's wrong?' or 'What's the problem?' you will be focused on just that - the problem. If, on the other hand, you ask 'What do I want?' or 'What do I want instead of this problem?' both your behaviour and your intentions are directed toward other possibilities or what you want instead of the problem.

A number of researchers and practitioners have spent time modelling this outcome-directed thinking process that is used by high performers across a variety of fields. This has included looking carefully at the thinking patterns, strategies and behaviours of eminent therapists, Olympic athletes, effective facilitators, managers, leaders and teams. They have found that a key to high performance across all these areas has been the ability to develop, state, and stay focused on a compelling outcome.

This research, as well as my own experience, has confirmed that outcome focussed thinking patterns are very learnable and applicable in any situation. They are, as you are probably already realising, fundamental to effective conversations. If you have a clear outcome it will enable you to stay focussed. It will also let the other person know where the conversation is going, and feel 'safe' about it as a result. In addition the conversation will focus on the issues that matter rather than letting the fog of other issues cloud a successful outcome

Try this ...

This is an exercise to see how outcome-directed thinking works.

Think of a problem that you have at work or home. For the purposes of this exercise, make the problem one that has been disconcerting, but not so overwhelming that you will have to drop this book and visit a therapist! On an emotional scale of 1-10, make the problem a 3-5.

The idea here is to experience both sets of questions and note the differences in your behaviour and in your feelings when you are answering them. Using the problem you selected above, answer the two sets of questions below either in your mind or on a sheet of paper. Simply answer the questions and pay attention to how you feel as you answer each question.

- Why do you have this problem?

- Who caused this problem?

- Who is to blame for this problem?

- What are the roadblocks or obstacles to solving this problem?

- How hopeful are you that this problem will be solved?

Now take a few seconds to remember what it felt like answering these questions. Next take a deep breath and with the same problem in mind, answer the second set of questions in your head.

- What do you want instead of this problem? (Your response will be your desired outcome.)

- How will you know you have achieved this outcome? What will you see, hear, and feel to know you have achieved this outcome?

- Imagine it is sometime in the future and you have the outcome you want. What have you gained by achieving this outcome? What have you lost?

- What resources will you have to use or get hold of to achieve this outcome?

- What is the first step you will take to achieve this outcome?

How Can Questions Provide Focus?

Take a few seconds now to notice how you were feeling and thinking when answering this second set of questions. Now compare your thinking process. How were your feelings and behaviour different between question sets I and II? What did you experience as you answered each set?

Most people say that they feel more positive when answering the second set of questions and that the first set of questions left them feeling 'stuck' and bogged down. Was this your experience? It is interesting that simply asking a few different questions can have such a powerful effect on our experience! Let's explore why this happened.

The first set of questions is representative of problem thinking.

Answering these problem questions directs your attention onto what is wrong, on the past history and background of the problem. Problem thinking keeps people focused on where they have been, a procedure that is tedious, difficult and generally leads to limited movement. It is like driving your car by looking through the rear-view mirror, always looking at where you have been and never really knowing where you are going!

Although questions like the first ones can be useful in clarifying a present problem situation, if all of one's efforts are focused only on the problem most people find that this results in low energy, discouragement, frustration, a sense of being 'stuck' and a lack of confidence that the problem can be solved.

Problem questions are what we were taught in school and are especially good for scientifically examining a problem. They are, as you can see, less helpful in conversations where we want to achieve a successful outcome. They are a habit we need to unlearn. By practising the second set and seeing the results, you will quickly be convinced of the benefits of making this change.

Outcome thinking, represented by the second set of questions, keeps people focused on what they want, or what they want instead of the problem. Rather than focusing on moving away from a problem, these outcome questions direct people to move positively toward what is wanted. Generally, using outcome-directed thinking makes you feel positive, motivated, full of energy and confident that the barriers or obstacles that might get in the way of a desired outcome can be removed. Rather than feeling stuck in a problem, the outcome thinking process helps us build useful, compelling, desired outcomes and helps create the actions and energy to accomplish them.

The key difference between problem and outcome-directed thinking is this ability to go for the outcome, to move toward a compelling desired state and not get stuck in the problem state, or simply move away from the problem. Another way to look at this is that the brain is an incredibly powerful honing mechanism. The brain will direct its energy and effort toward where we focus our attention. It will deploy all your resources to obtain what you want. If the outcomes are not clear, the brain gets confused. As you experienced in the exercise above, being focused on the outcome or being in the outcome frame is a much better place to be!

A few years ago I was having dinner with a colleague and an MP from a local constituency. He was asking me about the training courses I was running and in particular what I had been doing that day. I explained to him that one of the concepts I had been talking about was outcome thinking and told him what the concept was all about. He was interested and asked me how that may help with an open meeting he was hosting in his constituency the following day. He was expecting a lot of complaints and problems being raised about the particular issue they were dealing with. He wasn't looking forward to it as he felt it was going to be very negative and he would end up being very defensive.

So I advised him to listen, for a while at least, to the comments and complaints that people were making, as they needed to vent their feelings. However, after a while, he should stop and ask them what they wanted instead. Or, indeed, what they wanted him to do differently. This would get them to focus on what they wanted rather than complaining.

A few days later, after the meeting, he called me and said he had done exactly what I had advised him to do. He said that as soon as he asked the question the meeting went quiet for a while. People then responded by saying he should continue to do exactly what he was doing and that they had wanted him to know how they felt about the issue. He was amazed with the difference it made, both to him and to his audience.

So, if outcome thinking is as good as it says on the packet, let's have a look inside and examine it in a bit more detail. Outcome thinking:

- Helps us build useful, compelling, desired outcomes and helps create the actions and energy to accomplish them.

- Has a big impact on the responses you and others will make if you think about the outcome you want before responding to a situation

- Helps you and others understand at what level you can agree even if where you are seems a little blocked

- Helps define the outcome frame for a discussion – creating a 'safe' environment on both sides.

- Allows you to use outcome focussed questions to change the dynamics of a conversation

So let's examine each of these in turn.

Magnets, Purple Monkeys and Russian Dolls

It follows that if outcome thinking has this much impact on our focus and energy, then the more compelling the outcome and the better it is stated, the more impact it will have.

I use three ways to think about this. The law of threes is always a good one, as is making the heading for each slightly unusual. (I can still remember the planets in order from the sun by recalling the ridiculous line from my teacher 'Many volcanoes erupt mouldy jam sandwiches unless none provided'. How sad am I!) So here goes ...

Magnets – this is a metaphor for making the outcome so compelling you will be drawn towards achieving it.

I remember coaching someone who said to me his outcome was to be more organised. I thought, looking at his body language and energy, 'Yeah, right – I can see you are up for this'. So I asked '... and what will being more organised do for you?' He responded 'I would like to get to the end of the week thinking I had taken a step forward'. I could see his energy change as he was beginning to focus on what he really wanted.

So what makes an Olympic athlete train the hours they do in all weathers? It's because they see themselves on the podium being presented with the medal and knowing somewhere out there their mum, or nearest and dearest, is watching proudly. They visualise the success and imagine how it will feel and what they will see and hear. It becomes compelling to them.

So how many of your goals are truly compelling? And if they are not, how many of them do you achieve? Try and make them more compelling and think of what it will be like when you achieve them.

How Can Questions Provide Focus?

Benjamin Zander, renowned conductor of the Boston Philharmonic Orchestra, lecturer and conference speaker, tells his students at the beginning of the year 'I will guarantee you an 'A' at the end of the first term on one condition. You will write a letter to yourself as if from the end of the year, explaining how you achieved an end of year 'A' grade.' A great example of powerful outcome thinking

Trust your instincts, if the outcome doesn't feel right then it probably isn't right. Ask yourself the simple question: 'What would make it more compelling?' If it's not that compelling, it's unlikely you'll achieve it.

Purple Monkeys

OK a challenge for you. For the next 10 seconds do not think about purple monkeys ...... or documentaries about them...... or their mating habits ......

Did you manage? I doubt it. The brain somehow cannot fully comprehend the 'don't' bit. Just think of your kids playing in the garden .... you shout 'don't go behind the shed - my tools are there.' What happens? They think – the shed! That sounds interesting, and what happens a while later?

If you think about someone who says 'I'm going to give up smoking', what's the first thing they think of when they say that – smoking and cigarettes! Is that helpful when you are trying to give them up? There is even research to show that if you say to someone carrying a tray of glasses 'Mind you don't drop the tray!' the odds are that they actually will.

The Imp Of The Perverse - Edgar Allan Poe

'I would perpetually catch myself pondering upon my security, and repeating, in a low undertone, the phrase, I am Safe.

One day, whilst sauntering along the streets, I arrested myself in the act of murmuring, half aloud, these customary syllables. In a fit of petulance, I remodelled them thus I am safe, I am safe, yes, if I be not fool enough to make open confession!

No sooner had I spoken these words, than I felt an icy chill creep to my heart. I had had some experience in these fits of perversity, whose nature I have been at some trouble to explain, and I remembered well, that in no instance, I had successfully resisted their attacks.

And now my own casual self-suggestion, that I might possibly be fool enough to confess the murder of which I had been guilty, confronted me, as if the very ghost of him whom I had murdered, and beckoned me on to death.'

So the rule here is to **avoid purple monkeys**! (Of course you realise I have just given you one but very craftily!). State your outcome in terms of *what you want* rather than what you don't want. So if you want to give up smoking for example, think about what it will be like when you have given up (healthier, more attractive, wealthier, etc.) and frame your outcome around those positives.

Russian Dolls

We tend to achieve goals that are near and clear rather than those which are far and foggy. That doesn't mean to say that we can't have long-term goals, but we need to break them down into sub goals or sub outcomes. We need to get to the right sized chunk that is near enough and yet challenging enough for us to feel some urgency and yet have the belief that it is just about achievable

This can be quite a skill because if it seems too easy to achieve then there is a danger we think we can achieve it by just doing more of the same.

For example if I were to ask you to jump over a barrier three feet high, most reasonably able people could do it. If I asked you to come back in a week's time and get over a barrier three and a half feet high, what would you do in the intervening time? The answer most of us would give is practice and become a little fitter. If however I asked you to get over a barrier six feet high in a week's time, what would you do? Now you are probably thinking ladder, trampoline stilts, etc.

The difference in creating an outcome that is only just about achievable, means we have to think differently.

I have over the years witnessed many participants on my courses in one-to-ones practising difficult conversations with actors. They get into difficulties so we take a time out. I often ask 'What do really want to say here?' 'No one is about - just say it out loud.' It is then they come out with the compellingly urgent outcome such as 'What I want to say is if this guy doesn't get his act together he will soon be out of a job!'

Not only do they feel better having said this to themselves, but often by phrasing it a little better they have a compelling outcome that will achieve change.

This leads us on to another great benefit from adopting outcome thinking – the effect it has on your and others' responses.

Outcomes And Their Effect On Responses

Much of what we do in terms of the actions we take, the decisions we make and how we respond to challenges is based more on an automatic response to the circumstances at hand than to conscious choice. These responses are preconditioned from past experience or from our personality - but are not our only option.

Victor Frankl, a Jewish psychiatrist who was imprisoned in a concentration camp during the war, wrote of his discovery of what he called the 'ultimate human freedom'. One day, naked and all alone in a small room having just been tortured, he began to realise that while his captors could control his entire environment and could do what they wanted to his body, ultimately it was up to him to decide, within himself, how all of this was going to affect him. Between what happened to him, or the stimulus, and his response to it, was his freedom or power to choose his response.

We can often feel like victims and assume it is the other people who are difficult. This model is deceptively simple but very powerful. Take this simple example. Imagine that you'd agreed with your partner or a friend that you were going to cook them dinner at eight that evening. But they didn't turn up until ten, with no excuse and no phone call, and the dinner was ruined. That is the event – we can't change that. What reaction could you have in this situation? You could say, 'Your dinner is in the dog' or have a row and shout at them. Now of course if you reacted in that way, what might be the outcome - a miserable evening, one of those rows that last forever, lost friendship etc. In this situation we have allowed events to drive our outcome.

$$(E) vents + (R)eaction = (O)utcome$$

But what if you thought about the outcome you wanted before making the response. For example if your outcome were still to have a pleasant evening and remain friends with that person then you would think about the right response. You can still let them know you are unhappy but in a controlled way and perhaps ask them to go and get the takeaway and wine! Here you are far more in control of the outcome you want. Thinking about your outcome has tailored your response to meet it.

(E)vents + (O)utcome = (R)esponse

I think it's useful to think of a difference between the words 'reaction' and 'response'. A reaction is more emotional and immediate, while a response has more of a 'thought about' feel to it.

So this simple formula is very powerful. You can drive your own brain and not let others drive it for you. Starting to think in terms of the outcome you want gives you a much better chance of achieving it. As Victor Frankl showed, you are always in charge of your response and there are many ways to adjust it.

I remember a personal example of this. When running a programme, one of the modules covered outcome thinking. At the following module one of the participants took me aside at the first break to tell me this story. He got home from the last module to find the police outside his house. They had arrested his 15-year old son not only for taking drugs but also for dealing them. The police decided that as this was a first offence and for soft drugs they would caution and not charge his son. He said I was so angry my son had let me down and was about to let him know this in no uncertain terms when into his mind floated the concept of outcome thinking. He thought the outcome I want here is for this not to happen again. As soon as he thought this he calmed down and decided to have a real discussion with his son to understand why this had happened and how things needed to change. He said he had the best discussion with his son ever and was feeling this traumatic incident would now lead to a better relationship and far less chance of this behaviour in the future. Phew - powerful stuff eh!

It also leads to what I think is one of the most powerful questions you can ask anyone to change the dynamics of a conversation. When someone is complaining and in response mode ask:

What would you rather have?

or

What do you want instead?

Finding Agreement

Sometimes two people or groups appear to have different and seemingly irreconcilable outcomes. A specific historical example of this was the negotiation positions of Israel and Egypt after the six-day war. If you remember, Egypt and Syria had made a surprise attack on Israel. Israel, through a series of brilliant manoeuvres, not only repelled the attack but also gained Sinai. The new Egyptian president Sadat wanted peace brokered by the USA. The trouble was that Israel was refusing to give up Sinai and Egypt said it couldn't negotiate without the return of the territory - historically always theirs.

The way out was something we call chunking outcomes upwards by asking 'What does holding on to Sinai give you?' The answer from Israel was 'Security, security and security!' Egypt understood this and eventually the territory was given back to Egypt on the basis that it would always remain demilitarised. This is obviously a simplified version of what happened but in essence that was the difference that made the difference.

Outcomes can be 'chunked up' or 'chunked down' to get to the level of agreement or to get to specifics when agreement is vague

So if you want to 'chunk up' to a higher outcome, then ask:

What will having this outcome do for me/us?

How Can Questions Provide Focus?

And if you want to chunk down to a more specific outcome you can work on, ask:

What stops me/us from getting this outcome?

This latter question results in a problem or obstacle being identified. So to turn this into an outcome then ask the killer question:

What do I/we want instead?

Questions can be very useful for clarifying business goals and ensuring alignment of actions and goals down through the organisation. Many years ago I was lucky enough to visit Japan a few times. They are great lovers of baseball and when kids practice they often spend time throwing the ball to each other quickly for the other to catch it in the receiver's glove. They called this 'Catchball'. They also use this term to describe the way they cascade goals. It describes a participative process that uses iterative (throwing the ball back and fore) planning sessions to answer questions, clarify priorities, build consensus, and ensure that goals and measures are well understood, realistic and sufficient to achieve the overall objectives.

They use this process to cascade goals down though the organisation. What happens is that my actions (means) to achieve a higher-level goal then become the goals for the next level down. Everyone becomes clear and aligned and recognises their importance in achieving their goals.

So 'Catchball' in action uses the following process:

- Say your goal was in your sales team 'Increase sales by 10%'.

- You then ask each of your team members 'Assuming this is our goal, what actions would you propose to carry out to deliver it and what would that end result be?'

- Their answers to this question will enable you to check their understanding and discuss with them which actions may not be the right ones.

For example they could say that to achieve this goal they would spend more on advertising. This may not be what you want them to do. They may also come up with some new ideas you had not thought of that may lead you to increase your goal.

> *'A strategic plan is nothing but a dead letter. It comes to life only through discussion and negotiation.'*
>
> **President Dwight D. Eisenhower**

Not only are people clear on their goals but also on the journey: they develop their performance insight into how what they do impacts on achieving the larger goals.

So, in this section we have looked at how the importance of focusing on what you want rather than the problems you face is a much more positive energising process. It has a huge impact on the response of others. By following some simple rules we can help ourselves and others develop more powerful outcomes and clarify how their goals align.

The following summary of this chapter is followed by examples of great questions to ask. But, by simply having this approach in your mind, you will develop many others that will work for you.

How Can Questions Provide Focus?

So What Might We Have Learned From This Chapter?

1. What happens if you don't have an outcome focus?

2. What's the difference in having a powerful outcome compared with an OK one?

3. How useful is it to use outcome frame questions to change the dynamic of any conversation?

Top Ten Great Questions To Provide Focus

1. What would you rather have?

2. What do you want instead?

3. What specifically will having this outcome do for me/us?

4. What are the downsides?

5. On a scale of 1-10 how important is this to you and what would get it to ten?

6. What might it feel like when you have achieved this outcome?

7. What other benefits are there?

8. What will success look like?

9. What would be a good outcome for …?

10. What resources will you need to achieve this?

How Can Questions Manage Emotions?

In this chapter I will look at the role of emotions in our business lives. In understanding more how we all work emotionally, and what causes emotions to be triggered, it will provide the backdrop to the kinds of questions you can ask that will help you manage your own and other people's emotions more effectively

It is often said that we should get rid of emotions in business and just deal with the hard facts. The problem is that emotions are there for a purpose and are a key part of us. Emotions must be of some use, as they have been retained by the evolutionary process for millions of years. Instead of denying them or trying to hide them (impossible anyway) we should bring them into our conversations so that they can be the key to resolving things.

- Emotions are part of the conversation and they are telling us something

- Unless we deal with them they will limit our ability to resolve especially difficult interpersonal issues

- There are ways of managing our own and others' emotions to achieve better outcomes

We British are often known for not showing our emotions. We are known for keeping a 'stiff upper lip' and Roger Moore, the Bond film star, was known for showing his emotion by merely raising an eyebrow. Yet not all cultures are like this. I have some Italian friends who sound like the world is ending when they're arguing - lots of noise and shouting. And yet when they have finished they often give each other a hug and everything seems fine, even though those who witness it are often shocked for a while longer.

How Can Questions Manage Emotions?

Which culture is right? The fact is that emotions are at play in all cultures and all situations. They are telling us something and they are an essential element of a conversation. So we need to deal with them as part of our own conversations. How we deal with them may well be influenced by the cultures of which we are a part. However, there are some fundamental approaches that stand up and will increase our effectiveness in whatever culture or situation we are in.

One chapter of a favourite novel, 'The Help' by Kathryn Stockett, concludes with the words *'No one was speaking but there was definitely a conversation going on.'* Emotions are part of us and unless we manage, and to an extent control them, they will control and manage us.

What is the purpose of experiencing an emotion? When we feel an emotion it is triggering us to do something. When we feel frightened or angry we are motivated to do something. That something at its most basic level is to run away or to get ready to stand and fight - the flight or fight response. This was a very useful response in the early days of human evolution when many creatures were bigger and stronger than us, and we only had our wits to survive. While we still may fight or flee today, usually the response is more like hiding away, avoiding, becoming quiet - or becoming angry.

Emotions have a reason to be. They prompt us for action, they motivate us, help us communicate with others, and give us important information about what's going on in a given situation.

However like anything else in life, if misused or out of balance they can cause trouble. In that case, emotions can sometimes lead us to ineffective behaviours. Emotions can make you do things that you regret later and can cause trouble in different areas of your life. Unfortunately it's no good just suppressing them either. Research shows us time and time again that repressing emotions causes us internal stress and affects our physical and mental health

We need to learn to manage them more effectively so that we can learn to use them for our benefit

Emotions are a basic communication mechanism in our bodies and are primarily a chemical reaction. The chemical reactions are far faster than the electrical reactions of our nerves and are also generally far less specific. Although the feeling you are experiencing may not be suggesting a precise action, it is having a huge impact on how you react.

When I go to see a horror film (not something I often do), I am only frightened when I don't know exactly what it is I am frightened of. As soon as I know what it is (some strange horrible thing) I become significantly less frightened. It's a similar process with emotions.

As long as we are experiencing them, but not exactly aware of what we are experiencing and why, then they have control over us and everything we do. As soon as we begin to understand exactly what we are feeling and why, we begin to understand what the message really is and how we deal with it.

Consider for a moment the following scenario. You get up in the morning late because there was a problem with your alarm. Your kids have eaten all your usual breakfast cereal. You check the mail and find a large unexpected bill. On getting into your car you realise you are short of petrol. When you eventually arrive late at work you are angry and frustrated. Someone comes straight into your office complaining about what to you is a trivial response. What happens? There is a fair chance you might bite their heads off. Why? Because this emotion is overwhelming and controlling you. Normally you might well have handled this situation much more sympathetically.

In summary: emotions are powerful and almost immediate signals that we have to do something. They are usually related to:

Survival: Nature developed our emotions over millions of years of evolution. As a result, our emotions have the potential to serve us today as a delicate and sophisticated internal guidance system. Our emotions alert us when a natural human need is not being met. For example, when we feel lonely our need for connection with other people is unmet. When we feel afraid our need for safety is unmet. When we feel rejected, it is our need for acceptance that is unmet.

Motivation: Our emotions support us in achieving our goals. When we feel enthusiastic or passionate or excited about something, we are more likely to respond by taking action. When we are feeling sad or frustrated we know that we are far less likely to make things happen. Getting more in touch with those positive emotions is a powerful way of becoming more effective

Decision Making: Our emotions are a valuable source of information. Our emotions help us make decisions. Studies show that when a person's emotional connections are severed in the brain, he cannot make even simple decisions. Why? Because he doesn't know how he will feel about his choices.

Boundary Setting: When we feel uncomfortable with a person's behaviour, our emotions alert us. If we learn to trust our emotions and feel confident expressing ourselves, we can let the person know we feel uncomfortable as soon as we are aware of our feelings. This will help us set our boundaries, which are necessary to protect our physical and mental health.

Communication: Our emotions help us communicate with others. Our facial expressions, for example, can convey a wide range of emotions. If we look sad or hurt, we are signalling to others that we need their help. If we learn to express more of our emotional needs, we have a better chance of meeting them. If we are effective at listening to the emotional troubles of others, we are better able to help them feel understood, valued and cared about.

Happiness: It is self-evident that the only way we know that we are happy is when we feel happy. When we feel happy, we feel content and fulfilled. This feeling comes from having our needs met, particularly our emotional needs. We can be warm, comfortable, and full of food, but still unhappy. A friend whose wife had died told me, a year later, that he was able to experience enjoyment but not happiness. Our emotions and our feelings let us know when we are unhappy and when something is missing or needed. The better we can identify our emotions, the easier it will be to determine what is needed to be happy.

Unity: Our emotions are perhaps the greatest potential source for uniting everybody. Clearly, our various religious, cultural and political beliefs have not united us. Far too often, in fact, they have tragically and sometimes fatally divided us. Emotions, on the other hand, are universal. Charles Darwin wrote about this years ago in one of his lesser-known books 'The Expression of Emotion In Man and Animal'. The emotions of empathy, compassion, cooperation, and forgiveness, for instance, all have the potential to unite us as a species. It seems fair to say that, generally speaking: *Beliefs divide us. Emotions unite us.*

Emotions, then, are goal driven. They are signalling to us that a goal hasn't been met. The trouble is that they arise from the more primitive part of our brain that, in the early days of our evolution, gave us the basic drive to run or fight. While this was useful then, as we have evolved we have physically developed not to be able to fight so effectively (no claws or harp teeth) or run (less powerful limbs). So the reaction now becomes more of mental fight or flight. Mental flight usually translates into passive behaviour and mental fight into verbal aggression (although, unfortunately, we still engage in a fair amount of the physical kind too).

Evolution, however, has developed the thinking side of our brain: as we evolved we started thinking. So Og the caveman, when faced with a nasty sabre-toothed tiger, now starts to think rather than just fight

How Can Questions Manage Emotions?

or run. He thinks 'Cousin Ig tried to run and could not outrun tiger and was eaten. So that's no good. And cousin Ug tried to fight the tiger and failed and was eaten. So that won't work either'. So he reasons, 'Ah, but not seen tigers climb trees, so I climb tree fast'. Luckily he was able to adapt this thinking quite quickly or primitive man would not have survived and evolved from the clever Og and you would not be reading this today

But thinking is an electrical brain response not a chemical one, as emotions are, so it does take longer. It follows, therefore, that if you want good quality thinking it takes more time. Being assertive, rather than being aggressive or passive, takes time and is a learned skill and requires us to manage our emotions more effectively

There is also a relationship between these two areas of the brain. They are, what is known as *reciprocally inhibitive*. That's a mouthful meaning when one area is functioning it tends to switch the other off. If you are thinking you are doing little feeling. And when you are feeling you are doing little thinking. When emotions are too high, thinking is low. That's the source of our problems

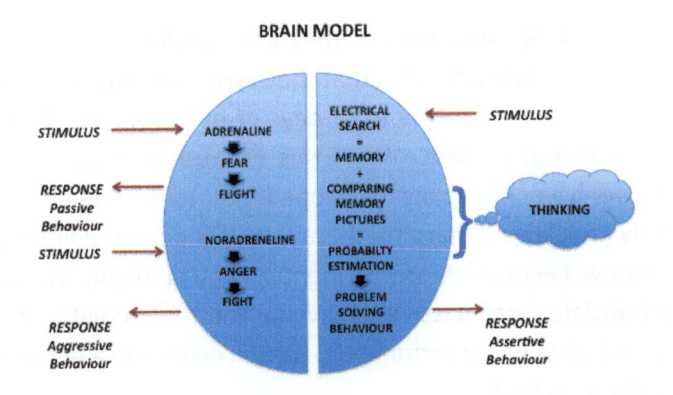

BRAIN MODEL

```
STIMULUS ──→  ADRENALINE       ELECTRICAL  ←── STIMULUS
                  ↓              SEARCH
                 FEAR              =
                  ↓              MEMORY
RESPONSE ←──   FLIGHT              +
Passive                         COMPARING
Behaviour                        MEMORY                THINKING
             NORADRENELINE       PICTURES
STIMULUS ──→     ↓                  =
                ANGER           PROBABILTY
                 ↓              ESTIMATION
                FIGHT               ↓
                                 PROBLEM
RESPONSE ←──                     SOLVING          ──→ RESPONSE
Aggressive                      BEHAVIOUR             Assertive
Behaviour                                             Behaviour
```

The good news is we can learn to become more in control of our emotions and also become more connected with them when we want to be. We can also learn to be more effective at helping others understand their emotions and use them more effectively.

The first step is awareness. Emotions have this nasty habit of clouding our judgement. You may be feeling sad, for example, because of something that has happened in your life. But this emotion also tends to spread its tentacles across all aspects of your life whether you want it to or not. Not only this, but research has shown that a negative emotional state will not only cloud your judgement at that moment, it will also store this emotional element with your memory of the decision, so you are likely to repeat the same poor decision time after time after time. And this will have happened to us without our realising that the original emotion arose from a far more limited situation.

Firstly we are all creatures of habit. Certain situations regularly trigger predictable reactions in us. Just for a moment, think about the emotional state triggered in you when a police car behind you on the motorway suddenly turns its blue flashing light on. A colleague of mine has two clients: one, an investment bank where employees dress formally and the décor is similarly severe; and the other, a creative media company where everyone dresses down and soft large cushions abound. What emotional state do you think is stimulated by each?

So, start to notice what triggers an emotional state in you. Is it useful or not? Where did it come from? How would you like it to be different? As thinking/feeling is to an extent reciprocally exclusive, when you start to recognise your emotion and what caused it, you engage the thinking part of your brain, which then naturally reduces the emotional part. It seems to me like the brain is trying to get a message through to you and once this has been recognised by the pre-frontal cortex (the thinking brain) it relaxes and says 'job done'.

As this process works for you it will also work for others. So if someone is behaving emotionally, ask what is causing them to feel that way. As soon as they respond, they too will engage the thinking brain and emotions will subside. So instead of having conversations that are filled with emotional behaviour we can have conversations where we recognise their impact and talk about them. We are talking about what we are feeling, not simply acting them out. We can have empathy and these emotional feelings become part of the conversation, as they should be.

What's important, it seems, is to become more aware of the actual emotion and get used to naming it. By doing so you can firstly understand the specific need it's addressing. Then, by the very fact that you become aware of it and name it, you are starting to engage the thinking side of your brain and naturally diminishing the impact of it. On the positive side, if it's a useful emotion like excitement or enthusiasm and you become aware of it, you can 'step into it' and use its positive effects more strongly.

I call this final point 'developing your emotional literacy'. I will now explore this aspect in more detail to see how we can use and exploit it

I define emotional literacy as the ability to express feelings with specific 'feeling' words, in 3-word sentences.

For example, 'I feel rejected.'

The purpose of developing our emotional literacy is precisely to identify and communicate our feelings. When we do this we are helping nature fulfil its design for our feelings. We must know how we feel in order to be able to meet our emotional needs. And we must communicate our feelings in order to get the emotional support and understanding we need from others, as well as to show our emotional support and understanding to them.

One of the first steps to developing our emotional intelligence is to improve our emotional literacy. In other words, to improve our ability to identify our feelings by their specific names - and the more specific we can be, the better. The first step of emotional intelligence is the capacity to perceive and to express feelings. Emotional intelligence cannot begin without the first step.

Although we have over 3,000 words in the English language that describe and identify our emotions, we simply don't use many of them. There are a lot of reasons why we don't make much use of this rich vocabulary. One is that we just aren't taught to speak using 'feeling' words.

I have found, though, that many people can identify their feelings quite well when given a little help. The first step is to start using simple, three-word sentences such as these:

- I feel sad.

- I feel motivated.

- I feel offended.

- I feel appreciated.

- I feel hurt.

- I feel disrespected.

And of course, if you are asking questions look for answers like this. This may feel strange at first, since not many people do this. But it gets easier with time.

When we talk about our feelings using three-word sentences we are sending what have been called 'I messages'. On the other hand when we say things like 'You make me so jealous' we are sending a 'you message'. These 'you messages' typically put the other person on the defensive, which harms communication and sours relationships rather than helping.

Note that when we say something similar to 'I feel like you...' we are sending a 'you message' in disguise as an 'I message'!

Some 'feeling' words not only express a feeling, but also express the intensity of the feeling. By expressing intensity, they communicate the degree to which our needs are being met and our values and beliefs are being upheld. Accurately capturing the intensity of an emotion is critical to judging the message our feelings are sending. If we exaggerate or minimize the feeling, we are distorting reality and undermining the effectiveness of our communication.

Here are a few ways to express verbally the intensity of a feeling

Weighting the feeling with a modifier

I feel a little hurt. I feel extremely hurt.

Choosing a specific word on the continuum of that emotion

I feel: annoyed... angry ... incensed...ballistic.

Making use of a 0 to 10 scale

I feel hurt 2 out of 10.

Of the three methods, the 0 - 10 scale is the one I like the best, especially if someone else is really interested in my feelings. It is also a great question to ask someone else:

On a scale of 1-10 how strongly do you feel about this?

Secondly, we know that emotions have a physical as well as a mental aspect. When we feel fear, for example, our bodies will often actually tremble and shake. When you see someone who is depressed you know they are from the way they are holding the bodies - their physiology.

What is not so well recognised is that it is not just a one-way process. That is, if you change your physiology or physical deportment, it will change your emotional state. For example try scrunching yourself up and looking at the floor while trying to feel happy. Similarly stretch yourself up and look at the sky and try and think miserable thoughts. Hard isn't it? So, if you want to feel differently, then act that way physically. As Marianne my colleague says, 'Fake it to make it'.

> People can forget what you said and what you did, but they nearly always remember how you made them feel
>
> **Maya Angelou**

Thirdly, if emotions are goal-directed it might help to understand what the goal is that you are focussing on - that which is causing a particular emotion. Is it reasonable? For example, if you believe that the person you are going to see is an aggressive SOB, then that will provoke a certain emotional reaction in you when you meet. So ask yourself ... 'Is he really that way?'

What stops us expressing our feelings?

Often, it is socially unacceptable directly to express certain emotions. We are too afraid of offending others, too afraid of appearing unhappy or unhealthy and too afraid of social disapproval. Sadly, we live in a world where appearances often matter more than reality. This seems to be especially true in the supposedly upper classes of society, where conformity and etiquette are considered to be so important.

So, instead of truthfully expressing our feelings clearly and directly, we express the same emotions indirectly, either through our actions or our body language. Sometimes we actually lie outright about our feelings. When we start to hide our feelings, or lie about them, or tell people only what we think they want to hear, we impede communication and distort reality.

Let's look at some examples of how we corrupt the language of feelings.

Masking. There are many ways we mask our real feelings. Sometimes we simply lie about them, for example when someone says she is 'fine', even though she is obviously irritated, worried, or stressed. Sometimes we intentionally or unintentionally substitute one feeling for another. For example, if I say 'I hope it doesn't rain,' we might actually be feeling afraid that it will!

Inconsistency. Often, our tone of voice or our body language contradicts the words we are actually using. None of us can entirely hide our true feelings, but many of us try to disguise our voices to go along with the act. People who are especially superficial even adopt the cosmetic voices found on television in order to further conform to societal expectations, and further mask their true feelings.

Overuse. One of the ways we corrupt language is to over-use a word. Consider the word 'love.' We love ice cream, beer, apple pie, and our mothers. Doesn't it seem there should be a different word for the way we feel about our parents as opposed to food?

'Hate' is another word that is greatly overused. If someone hates traffic, hates cabbage and hates bankers, how can they express their feelings about child abuse?

Exaggeration. When we exaggerate our feelings we are being deceitful in order to get attention. People who need to exaggerate have probably had their feelings ignored for so long that they have resorted to being dramatic to be noticed and valued. Unfortunately, when they send out false signals they alienate people and risk becoming like the boy who cried wolf. If you send out too many false alarms, you might be ignored when you truly need help.

Consider these exclamations, none of which are typically true in a literal sense but are examples of being over-dramatic:

I feel mortified. I feel devastated. I feel crushed. I feel decimated. I felt run over by a truck.

Minimization. Many people minimize their feelings, particularly when they are upset, worried or depressed. They use expressions such as:

I'm fine. I'll be all right. I'm ok, don't worry about me. There is nothing wrong. I said I was fine.

Such people typically are either too proud, too stubborn, too scared, or feel too unworthy to share their feelings. They desperately need to be connected with others, but they will not allow others to get close to them. They effectively push people away by withholding their true feelings. As a result it's very hard to establish a connection with them

Many years ago I had some counselling – a great experience. I said to my coach that I was a pretty optimistic sort of person and always looked for the positives in life. But I admitted that I got fed up when people said I was so lucky to be so positive all the time. I said 'I get fed up and depressed at times too, but they never seem to notice'. She said 'What do you reply when someone asks you how you are?' I said 'Fine'. And she replied 'Well, how will they ever know and what more can they say?' So now, if I'm stressed, I might say 'I'm fine - it's been a stressful week, though'. And in so doing, I've offered them a follow-up question and encouraged conversation.

Because we are not skilled at directly expressing our feelings, we often resort to indirect communication such as using examples, figures of speech and non-verbal communication. Let's look at a few of these forms of indirect communication.

I Feel Like....

Using sentences that begin with 'I feel like...' may be the most common method of communicating our feelings. But the literal result is that we often 'feel like' labels, thoughts or behaviours.

I feel like (a label). In the following examples we are labelling ourselves and not clearly and directly expressing our feelings.

I feel like: ... an idiot ... a baby ... a failure

Typically we use lots of expressions that put ourselves down. These negative labels certainly don't help us feel any better about ourselves. In fact, by mentally branding us, they make it more likely we will repeat the exact kinds of action that caused our feelings.

I feel like (a thought). In these examples we are actually conveying more of a thought than a feeling.

I feel like you are crazy. I feel like it was wrong. I feel like he is going to win.

I recall a conversation when I asked someone how she felt about something and she said 'I feel like you shouldn't have done that.' At another point when I asked about her feelings, she said, 'I don't want to get into all of that.' Such a lack of emotional literacy and emotional honesty makes it difficult to have a relationship, even a friendship or a working relationship.

I feel like (a behaviour). Here, we are expressing our feelings in the form of behaviour. Again, these are unclear and indirect. They may be graphic and entertaining but they are usually exaggerations and distortions that don't help us focus on our true feelings.

I feel like ... strangling him ... shooting him ... wringing his neck ... telling her off ... teaching him a lesson ... filing for divorce ... dumping him ... quitting ... giving up ... jumping off of a cliff

In other words, people who use expressions such as feeling like a behaviour, an action or an act are not in touch with their feelings. They may be acting out their lives as they think others would want them to, rather than acting as unique individuals. Or they simply imagine themselves taking action rather than actually using their emotions to motivate them to take appropriate action.

Don't do something permanently stupid because you are temporarily upset.

Anon

In his great book 'Non Violent Communication' Marshall Rosenburg demonstrates that an emotional reaction is at its core linked to a need that is not being met. When a need is not being met we react and then, as we have shown, we begin acting out that emotion and taking up unreasonable positions. People then find it very difficult to budge from such positions.

This offers us a clue that will help us engage in both a reasonable and safe conversation. We can ask people about their feelings and what is making them feel so strongly about something. This may well uncover needs that aren't being met (or they believe are not being met) and by holding a conversation, by asking questions, we can identify what needs are not being met and what should happen for them to be met.

Emotions are always part of the conversation. You may not be expressing them verbally, or think you are not non-verbally, but they will always leak out and they are often the 'elephant in the room'. By recognising the lessons in this chapter and putting them into practice,

How Can Questions Manage Emotions?

emotions can form a valuable part of the conversation where they belong.

Using Questions to Help Manage Emotions

From this section I hope you can begin to see where asking a powerful question, either of yourself or of another person, may help to uncover what's really going on. The best type of questions, to help manage both our own and other people's emotions in a conversation, would be those that help you and others to:

- Realise what emotion you or they are experiencing so that it becomes more explicit for you / them. As we have uncovered already, doing so straight away engages the brain in a more rational way.

- Understand what needs they or you have that are not be being met. Once these are uncovered a much more reasonable conversation can take place.

- Use the right language to talk about emotions and own them rather than blame them on someone else.

What Might You Have Learned In This Chapter?

- How useful is it to be analytically aware of your own feelings?
- What will happen when you ask others how they are feeling?
- What is the link between body and mind and what should you do about it?
- Why is it powerful to own your emotions and use 'I' not 'You'?

Top 10 Questions To Help You To Manage Emotions More Effectively

- How are you feeling about this?
- What is making you feel so strongly (passionately) about this?
- I notice you feel strongly about this, tell me what that's about?
- What needs to happen to resolve this?
- How has …. led you to feel that way?
- What, specifically, are you feeling?
- How do you think the other person is feeling about this?
- How long have you felt this way?
- On a scale of 1-10 how strongly do you feel about this?
- What has triggered this feeling?

How Can Questions Build Self-Awareness?

A poor life this if, full of care, we have no time to stand and stare.

William Henry Davies

It is all very well, you might say, to think about the outcomes I want before I act, or to challenge assumptions, or analyse my emotions and those of others. When we are in the hurly burly of modern day living, with all the demands on our time and all the distractions we face, when do I have the time or space to think like this?

This is made worse by the fact that much of our behaviour is habitual. We don't even think about it. You probably got up today and followed the same routine, drove the same way to work and probably didn't even remember much of the journey. Habits are very useful. Our Cerebral Cortex, the brain's executive function, can only cope with so much at a time. If we had to think about walking in order to walk, our brains wouldn't have much space or energy for much else.

We know we are capable of better. So why do we make so many short-sighted, thoroughly bad decisions? Most of us aren't aware that we each have at least two very distinct selves. These identities don't know very much about one another. If you doubt this is so, think about what you're like at your best and what you're like at your worst. Which one is the real you? The answer, of course, is both - two selves - both you.

Under ordinary circumstances, our parasympathetic (zombie) nervous system and our prefrontal cortex (the thinking bit) are running the show. We're capable of thinking clearly, calmly and logically. It's here that we're capable of operating at our best.

However, in the face of a perceived threat, our sympathetic (trigger) nervous system and amygdala (emotional memory bit) take over and our second self steps up. A flood of stress hormones is released. Our pre-frontal cortex shuts down, we become narrow and more myopic in our vision and we react more primitively and instinctively. The physiology of fight or flight mobilises us to attack - or run like hell!

This is our 'Survival Zone.' It's a great place to be if there's a lion coming at you. It isn't great in situations where thinking is an asset. The problem is that our bodies respond to any perceived threat - a critical comment from a colleague or a boss, for example - by fuelling the fight or flight response. We lose our capacity for rationality and reflectiveness and (worst of all) we probably don't realise we've lost it.

Consider a classic question you've surely asked someone, or been asked yourself:

> 'What were you thinking when you did that?'

More often than not, you weren't thinking anything at all. You were just reacting.

Our lives become so busy that we don't have time to stop and reflect on why we are doing what we are doing. I once interrupted a CEO I was working with, who was explaining how his strategy had been cascaded into action plans and targets and measures and so on, with the simple question 'What future does your strategy assume?' I only interrupted him because it was unclear to me. He had been so absorbed in the momentum of his wonderful strategic plan (and it was beautiful), that he had not stopped to consider whether the future he was assuming his plan would be addressing would indeed come to be.

Imagine a sports car without brakes! Some people find it very difficult to slow down their thinking, especially when momentum has been allowed to build. Our minds can easily become like very fast cars with

How Can Questions Build Self-Awareness?

great engines and accelerators, but poor sets of brakes. When we are running on adrenaline generated by one crisis after another, it can be very hard to find, much less want to apply, the brakes. Yet, when driving a car there are, of course, many occasions where the ability to stop is certainly as important as the ability to go! It's very useful to have a mental engine that can do both and that responds to the wishes of you, the driver. The faster my car, the more important it is that I know how to slow it down.

Remember the example we talked about under emotions. It's the start of a bad hair day. You wake up late. Your favourite breakfast cereal has run out. In the post is an unexpected and unplanned for bill. Your car is low on petrol and needs refilling on the way to work, making you late. You hit unexpected road works. You get to work and have to rush straight into a meeting, which then goes badly.

Then, returning to your office, someone makes what might normally be a fairly innocuous request - and you bite his or her head off. You get back to the office feeling even worse.

It's a bit like the domino effect. We allow a mixture of past events and habitual responses to get us in a mess with our thinking and actions because we don't stop and think. We allow others to drive our brains for us

Daily momentum is like being part of a medieval army fighting off an enemy with swords in a valley. While you are engaged in active fighting your focus is very narrow. You are preoccupied with the immediate threats and opportunities within a few meters of where you are fighting. Perhaps you are fully engaged with the person you are actually fighting and only vaguely aware of one or two potential foes, or of your compatriots, fighting near to you. The demands of the immediate situation take all your attention - as I guess they should.

Now imagine that you take a few moments to disengage from the action and move a few steps up the hillside. Immediately, two things happen. First, you are removed from both the threats and challenges of the fight with all its physical and mental intensity. Secondly, your perspective has changed. From your more elevated position, you have the advantage of a wider point of view. Instead of being aware of only a few soldiers, you may be able to see your entire company. With this new perspective, you may see where someone needs your help or where there is an advantage to be taken, and you can change your tactics accordingly.

If you allowed yourself the time to take a few more steps up the hillside, your view would be further expanded and perhaps you could view the situation of your entire division. And if you went to the very top of the hillside, you could view the entire valley and gain a strategic view of both armies at once. The increased distance from the battle would give you a wider perspective and the ability to make clearer choices. If you decide that this is a battle worth fighting, you could decide where you could make your best contribution and then re-engage in the battle with clarity and a renewed sense of purpose.

I once attended a talk by Deepak Chopra and he offered this analogy. Imagine a lake, very still and calm. If you dropped a pebble into it you would notice every ripple. But for most of us, our minds are like the North Atlantic in a storm. You could drop the Empire State building into it and we wouldn't notice.

Remember the last time you pushed the 'send' button for an email and then instantly regretted it, or snapped at someone in a moment of frustration? It's easy to recall all we do wrong in our lives - eat and drink too much, exercise and sleep too little, buy things we don't need, judge others too quickly.

STOP, a term coined by Timothy Galwey in his 'Inner Game' books, is a simple technique that allows us to apply the brakes, that permits us to take that walk up the hillside - and, as a result, to act more clearly and effectively.

He simply states that, not only should we stop and draw breath and think when we are in the middle of a crisis, we should make a habit of doing this *before* we experience problems to avoid the momentum building up

So making breaks during the day when you can STOP, however artificial they may seem, is absolutely vital for you to be at your best. So participants on my programmes have come up with some of the following ideas:

- Park you car in the furthest space in the car park from your office so, as you walk in, you can get your mind straight.

- Plan your meetings so that there is space between them.

- Walk around the office or factory every now and then.

- Make sure you have a proper coffee or lunch break.

Timothy Galwey states that: 'Thousands of managers from many different companies have agreed that STOP has become an indispensable tool for working effectively. One manager called it the 'tool of all tools' because, as he said, 'this is the tool that helps you remember to use all the other tools you have in your arsenal.'

Step back

Think

Organize your thoughts

Proceed

To step back means to put distance between yourself and whatever you are involved with at the moment. Step back from the momentum of action, emotion, and thinking. Step back and collect yourself. Find a place of balance and poise – a place where you can think clearly, creatively, and independently.

STOPs can be of any duration. A short STOP may last no more than a couple of seconds. For example, the phone rings while you are working on a project. Your hand reaches out as if of its own volition to answer the phone. A two-second STOP allows you to ask yourself if you really want to answer the phone at this moment. The STOP doesn't imply a correct answer, it just creates the opportunity to put you back in the driver's seat. Medium STOPs allow time to reflect and evaluate a situation before proceeding into action. Despite the popular Nike advert that recommends 'Just do it,' just doing it without stopping to consider options and consequences usually results in a lot of 'just undoing it'. And every once in a while, you can take a big STOP to give yourself the chance to look at issues from a more strategic perspective.

Here are some examples of short to medium STOPs:

With any communication, STOP, before you speak. Is every thought that comes to mind worthy of coming out of the mouth? STOP allows us to screen our thoughts for appropriate content, timing, and conciseness. Similarly, not everything we hear is fit to digest. Use STOP as a filter to discriminate between what is and is not necessary to take to heart.

You arrive at your desk and notice a few papers that have not been dealt with. Does your hand reach out automatically to pick them up, or do you STOP to consider your priorities for the day first, the most important of which may not be as visible as the papers?

How Can Questions Build Self-Awareness?

A fellow worker starts complaining. You know he is the kind of person who likes complaining but never does anything about the problem. He's asking for your agreement with his complaint. Do you STOP or jump in with your opinion without thinking whether or not you want to go down that road with him?

You find yourself feeling pressured and stressed by your workload and you realize that in this state you cannot give your best thinking to the task at hand. You know you are making little mistakes. Do you STOP and take a break or power through?

A colleague is asking you a question. Before he is finished, your mind has already come up with an answer to the question you *think* she is about to ask. Does this answer come out of your mouth before she has finished, or do you stop the mental momentum to fully hear what is being asked and consider your reply?

How many times in a single workday do you have to interrupt what you are doing to start something else? You may even stop something important to take care of a time-sensitive but less important task. In my workday, there can easily be more than twenty such 'interruptions.' Each interruption brings an automatic reaction of annoyance and with it a loss of conscious mobility.

The alternative is to STOP first and make a conscious choice about if and when to interrupt what you are doing. This STOP doesn't take away the consequences of the interruption, but it allows me to exercise my choice. It removes the annoyance and provides a sense of freedom and enjoyment because I still have my hands on the steering wheel of my workday. If I decide yes, then before starting the new activity, I take a short STOP to consciously 'close the books' on the last activity and to orient myself to the purpose and context of the next.

One tip for buying yourself some time, when you need to have an unplanned STOP in that moment when you notice that things are going wrong, is not to react but to ask a question. Ask for more information, or why someone is feeling so strongly about something, or just to clarify what is going on. This will give you just that little space to start your thinking brain working.

Once you have stepped back you can then think.

- What outcome do I want here?
- How am I feeling?
- How might another person be feeling?
- What's going on for the other person?
- What assumptions are getting in the way?

You can then organise your thoughts and decide how to proceed.

So, taking time to reflect is a vital activity. Recent research from neuroscience has confirmed that we know instinctively that it is when we have time to reflect that we get real insight and learning. The brain needs time to calm down and sort things into the right places and make new connections.

Neuroscience also tells us that once past adolescence, we don't so much make new memories or neural pathways, rather we recall old memories and try to connect them to new experiences and information. It seems that if we cannot connect, then it is unlikely that new information or experience will get filed away very efficiently, and may soon get lost.

In 1949, Donald Hebb, a Canadian neuropsychologist, wrote what has become known as Hebb's Law: 'Neurons that fire together wire together.' Each experience we encounter, whether a feeling, a thought, a sensation (and especially those that we are not aware of) is embedded in thousands of neurons that form a network (net). Repeated experiences become increasingly embedded in this net, making it easier for the neurons to fire (respond to the experience) and more difficult to unwire or rewire them to respond differently.

This is a good thing when learning the name of a new acquaintance - the net helps us to remember. But not so good when being yelled at repeatedly as a child - the net also remembers this and has a difficult time knowing how to respond later in life when someone raises their voice with us. Renewing our minds is all about creating new, healthy nets that fire together so they can wire together.

So taking time to stop and reflect is vital. When you are in that state you can then ask yourself and others questions which can reveal more about what is really going on. If you are to become better at asking questions, this ability to think before acting is essential. We need to get out of the habit of acting on impulse and act more on purpose

Some of the questions that you can use here are ones that initially can help you just do the standing back bit. Some of them will be those you can ask of yourself when you have become more reflective and self-aware.

What Might You Have Learned In This Chapter?

- How important is it to take time to stop and reflect?

- To what extent are you driven by events and what might be the benefits of changing your approach?

- What ways could you find of building STOP moments into your life?

Top 10 Questions To Help You To Become More Self Aware

1. What were you thinking when you did that?

2. What would need to happen to be the best you could be?

3. What's the story I'm telling myself here and how could I tell a more hopeful and empowering story about this same set of facts?

4. What if I'm wrong?

5. What will happen if you do change?

6. What will happen if you don't change?

7. What won't happen if you do change?

8. What won't happen if you don't change?

9. If you could make one change in your life, what would it be?

10. What needs to happen next?

How Can Questions Challenge Assumptions?

Our Assumptions

Whether you believe you can, or whether you believe you can't, you're probably right.

Henry Ford

We all have to make assumptions to get by in the world. If we had to consider everything from first principles we would never get anything done. So when we observe anything and store it away in our memories, we store with it the context as we see it, together with our emotions and certain assumptions about what this means.

So, for example, when we see an individual dominating a meeting and not allowing others to contribute, we might store how we felt about that person and consider that he or she is potentially difficult to deal with. When we next have dealings with them, we recall that memory together with the assumption that they are difficult to deal with.

How might you behave with someone you believed was like that? I suspect you might be more careful, guarded and defensive - or even offensive.

Now, how might they react to your behaviour? Again I suspect it would be just as difficult, guarded, defensive or even offensive. And so the meeting doesn't go well and your assumption that they were difficult is reinforced.

The trouble is that the assumption you made originally might have been wrong, or the person might have been having a bad day. What if you had assumed instead that they were passionate and an expert on the subject?

One Friday night, when I was in the waiting area of our local hospital's emergency room, an ambulance arrived. The crew wheeled in a stretcher carrying a young teenage driver who was looking quite pale. As the ER physician came out to meet them, the crew explained the teen had been in a bad car accident and had lost a considerable amount of blood. The ER physician gave the boy a quick once over and said, 'He needs to get into surgery immediately. But I can't operate on him, he's my son!'

Here's a brainteaser. The physician, who was not the boy's father, was telling the truth. Who was the physician?

If you think long enough about this story you will realise that one flawed assumption is blocking you (by the way, the answer's at the end of the chapter!).

I frequently find that people unwittingly prevent themselves from achieving their goals and dreams because of seemingly logical, but actually faulty, assumptions. If you're like most people, you're probably unwittingly thwarting yourself from attaining some of your goals, too.

Isn't it obvious that you're falling into an 'assumption trap'? No, not when they're your own faulty assumptions. It's much easier to spot other people's assumptions. Have you ever watched someone getting increasingly frustrated trying to push a door open that you know needs to be pulled? All it takes is one inaccurate belief to stop the person from getting through the doorway. Once the error is realised, the person can open the door easily. Assumptions are always based on our best logic. In turn, that logic is a combination of personal experience and the information available. Faulty logic will produce incorrect assumptions. At times, incorrect assumptions can have serious consequences. Even a single faulty assumption can turn an opportunity into an unsolvable problem.

How Can Questions Challenge Assumptions?

This is made worse by the fact that when we act in accordance with our assumptions, people react to the way we act and, hey presto, our assumptions become self-fulfilling.

The trouble is that not all the assumptions we make are either true or helpful. Because of the way our brains work, whenever we see something we start to do some pruning and reshaping of what we saw.

For example, a little while ago I was facilitating a project team though a difficult morning when there had been many differing views expressed. We were finally coming to a common goal and approach when one of the team suddenly said 'I think we've reached breaking point.' My frustration after a difficult morning initially failed to see all the positive body language that went with these words and I was just about to say what I thought about his behaviour when 'good facilitator' training took hold. So I asked him what he meant by that. His reply was that it had indeed been a difficult morning and what he meant was that we were about to achieve a breakthrough!

Not only can we make the wrong assumptions about things, but these assumptions can then affect our behaviour as a result. This process is what Peter Senge calls 'climbing up the ladder of inference':

WE SEE SOMETHING

WE DISTORT, CHANGE, AND MISS SOME OF WHAT WE SAW

WE MAKE ASSUMPTIONS BASED ON THIS

WE ACT ON THOSE ASSUMPTIONS

PEOPLE REACT TO THE WAY WE REACT

THESE ASSUMPTIONS BECOME SELF-FULFILLING!

Let me give you an example. In our daily lives, driving around town we are often delayed by crews, usually of men, digging holes in the road. When we eventually pass them, what do we see going on? I know this is a generalisation, but they don't seem to be working very hard. You know the image: one man digging and two others watching while a fourth makes the tea. So if, like me, you see this image, what conclusions are you tending to draw about their motivation and their interest in the quality of what they are doing? Well, when I ask groups this they will say they are probably lazy, work shy and not much interested in quality.

Now imagine you are the boss of several of these work crews, all dotted around the city so you cannot possibly be with all of them all of the time. How would you typically manage a group with these assumed attributes? Again, most people say they would constantly check on them, check their work, pay them surprise visits, pay them for what they do rather than the time they spend, etc.

Now put yourself in the shoes of one of these crews who had a boss who behaves like this. How would you react and behave? I suspect you would become de-motivated and try and get away with as much as you can.

So here's the rub:

- I drew assumptions from what I saw.
- I acted in accordance with those assumptions
- They reacted to how I acted,
- My assumption became self-fulfilling.

And it was all based on an assumption, which could be easily challenged. Is it manifestly true, for example, that every work crew everywhere is lazy and has to be managed this way? In my consulting career, as part of an assignment I once spent time with a group of engineers working to maintain overhead power lines. Naturally they wanted to ensure that the power was switched off before they started! They could not get confirmation of this for most of the day and had little choice but to sit around. When their supervisor visited later in the day he told them they would have to wait but could they ensure they hid themselves from passers by!

In a piece of research I read a few years back, researchers took a group of unemployed people who were to be trained as welders and divided them into two groups to be trained by the same instructor. The instructor was told that one group had passed an aptitude test for welding while the other group had failed. In fact this was untrue. The groups had been selected at random. Which group got the best results? I'll leave you to work it out. (How do they get permission to do these studies I wonder!)

So assumptions have an impact on how we think about things. They have an impact on:

What we believe is possible and what we believe is not. And yet they may not be true. In fact if you try hard enough you can find evidence to support most assumptions – try it. The question is not whether they are true, it's whether they are useful. A couple of years ago a colleague and I, after much difficulty and persistence, had arranged an appointment with the HR Director of a company we believed we might be able to do business with. On the way there we got caught in bad traffic and eventually arrived almost an hour late. The client came down to reception and I apologised for the fact we were almost an hour late. He replied that in fact we were 23 hours early. We had come a day early! He said he would try to re-arrange things so that he could still give us time, and he left to do so. I suggested to my colleague that having messed up after all the effort we had gone to, we now stood little chance of getting work from him. To which my wise colleague, John, said 'Well, you could assume that or you could assume that because he has gone away to rearrange his day to see us he must think it's worth it.' Either assumption could be true – I choose the latter and felt better. (We still didn't get any work by the way!)

Our attitude towards other people. Try this little exercise for instance. Listen to someone, maybe on television, and assume that they really know what they are talking about and you trust them completely. Now try to do the same but with the opposite belief. I often do this, working in pairs at workshops. I ask the designated speaker to identify what the listener was assuming - and they guess correctly. Your beliefs and assumptions leak out!

Conflict between people will often arise because we are not aware of, or are not expressing, our underlying assumptions and beliefs. All of our actions are based on assumptions - some are positive and true, some are negative and untrue. We don't need to remove positive ones. We're looking for obstructive or 'blocking' assumptions. We need to search for and remove these assumptions to free up thinking for individuals, groups and whole organisations.

Sticking to our assumptions *no matter what* allows us to perpetuate grudges and to hold on to the way we've always done things, even if we sometimes end up feeling like a victim and even if it is counter-productive and leads to inaction. Our assumptions convince us that we are right - and anyone who sees things differently is therefore wrong. And it feels good to be right. A good assumption to make is that all my assumptions could be wrong, or if they are not wrong then probably they're not useful.

So let's examine these two impacts in more detail in terms of how they affect our interactions with others and how, once we become aware of them, we can find more useful assumptions to unfetter us.

Getting Rid Of Blocking Assumptions

We make assumptions about what is possible for us, what is not, what the 'rules' are etc. These assumptions limit what we do even though they may be untrue.

I make an assumption for myself that I find really useful:

'All my assumptions are probably untrue.'

This helps me examine all the assumptions I make.

When Edmund Hillary was about to make his final ascent of Everest, some members of his team looked up at the summit and said that it was impossible. Hillary looked up and said 'It's going to be difficult, but not impossible'. If you think about this, you can see that Hillary had an in-built assumption in what he said.

How do we identify and remove these limiting or unhelpful assumptions?

When you identify something that appears to be limiting, you can ask a question that will help to move you from that which has been expressed to the underlying assumption.

Ask: *'What are you assuming that possibly stops you from doing what you want to do?'*

When you have identified the limiting assumption, you can then ask what Nancy Klein in her book 'Time To Think' calls the 'incisive question'. This is the one that removes and changes a limiting assumption. In phrasing this incisive question, you have to develop a more freeing assumption. However, at this stage you do not have to believe it.

A good way to start is simply to take the opposite of the limiting assumption. For example, instead of 'I don't have the right to raise this issue' simply change it to 'I *do* have the right to raise this issue'. Now, when you ask the incisive question, let go of your previous beliefs and assume that just for the purposes of this process - wild and wacky though it may seem - you knew this more freeing assumption was true. What would it do for you, and what might be happening differently?

The Incisive Question

If you knew the opposite to be true for you, what would you be doing, or what would be happening, differently? For example: 'If you knew that you have the right to raise this issue, what would you be doing?' or 'If you knew that you have the right to raise this issue, what would change for you?'

Changing Assumptions / Beliefs Exercise

1. Identify a specific area you want to work on.

2. What are some of the beliefs and messages you have about the issue you've chosen?

3. What would you like to be possible for you in relation to this issue? Phrase this as an objective in about half-a-dozen words.

4. Which is the main belief or message that you feel stops you achieving your objective?

How Can Questions Challenge Assumptions?

5. Explore your limiting assumption in more detail.

    a. How does this assumption affect your behaviour?

    b. How does it serve or help you?

    c. What does it prevent you from seeing or doing about yourself and others?

    d. How long have you had it?

    e. How strong is it?

    f. What would be a freeing assumption for you?

6. Note your Incisive Question here: If I knew that……..

Sample Incisive Questions

- If you knew that you are at least as intelligent as anyone else, what would you change for you?

- If you knew you have choices you have not yet considered, what would you face that you have been denying?

- If you knew you are good enough, what would you do and how would you feel?

- If you knew you are worthy of the best, what would you want?

- If you knew working hard is not the same as working well, how would you approach your work differently?

- If you knew you are significant in the world, what would change for you?

- If you thought of yourself as a leader, what would you most enjoy leading?

- If you were not holding back, what would you be doing?

- If you could make one change in your life, what would it be?

- If you were not afraid, what would you do?

- For things to be exactly right for you, what would have to change?

- If you began to care more about what you think than about what other people think of you, what would you think and do?

Reassessing The Assumptions We Make About Others

It is easy to see how the assumptions we make about people can inhibit our dealings with them. If you assume someone is going to be difficult, you are likely to be tense and a bit 'prickly', ready to interpret what you see as evidence of how difficult they are to deal with. That energy is likely to be picked up by the other person and as a result they may become tense, prickly and – yes, in your view – difficult. QED!

Now I am not arguing here that some people sometimes do behave in what seem to us strange and difficult ways. Sometimes, we may decide there are too many other issues and too little time, and decide to ignore them or what they have said. However if we want to change the dynamics of a relationship, then it's up to us to try something different to see if we can get another result

So how do we change our assumptions about others? It's pretty difficult to go from 'she's difficult' to 'she's wonderful'. You might find that hard to believe and as a result you would end up acting rather than engaging in real behaviour change. Acting takes effort and usually won't look convincing.

The first thing to do is to re-examine the assumptions you are making about that person and identify more useful ones that you can believe. I can think of no more powerful way of doing this than by asking the following question:

What would make a reasonable person act in this way?

Just stop for a moment. Think of someone you think of as difficult in some way and ask yourself this question about him or her. I am willing to bet you started to think of some other reasons (assumptions too but probably more useful ones) that explained their behaviour.

I was having a private meeting to discuss a report I had produced for the CEO of a distribution company, a long-standing client of mine, about the problems he was having with his business. I spent about an hour telling him what was going wrong. When I had finished he said 'Thanks for that and we have a lot to do. But you won't be able to be involved in the next phase because you will obviously have upset a lot of people in going about this'.

I was shocked and a little upset but managed to keep a lid on it. I said that that was a shame but suggested we discuss the action plan going forward. Then, by asking myself what would make a reasonable person behave in that way, I realised that this man, who I considered to be a friend, was feeling pretty bad about things and that his outburst may well have been due to this. I decided to continue calmly discussing things and later said I was disappointed not to be able to help further directly, but was willing to offer any indirect help he needed.

He responded by apologising for his earlier remarks and of course I had to be involved. Thank god I didn't react immediately and allowed myself time to check what I might be assuming.

So what this question does, just for a moment at least, is to suspend all the limiting assumptions that you are making and to assume that they are, underneath, a reasonable person. Sometimes it's hard to do even this, but if you don't do it you are likely to be locked into an assumption trap and be unable to improve that working relationship.

Reframing

Another way of helping people look at something in a different way is to ask questions that will possibly make them view the same situation in a different light. This is often called re-framing. Just imagine how the famous portrait of the Mona Lisa would look in a pink plastic frame!

Changing the frame of an experience can have a major influence on how you perceive, interpret and react to that experience. Being told that you have one hour to complete a task will most likely result in a different emotional state, approach and quality of work, than if you are told that you have one week to accomplish the same task. This illustrates how a change in frame (in this case a time frame) can have a significant impact on the choices you make.

The purpose of reframing is to help a person experience their actions, the impact of their beliefs, etc. from a different perspective (frame) and potentially to be more resourceful or have more choice in how they react. They may then make a different set of assumptions. Some typical types of reframes are as follows:

- Politicians are masters at reframing. It seems no matter what happens, they can put a positive spin on it for themselves or a negative spin for their opponents.

- You may be frustrated at your wife for inviting the elderly gentleman next door for supper. Until she points out that if

How Can Questions Challenge Assumptions?

you were in his shoes, then you may find this simple act to be the highlight of your week.

- Consider that old wooden table in the basement that you use as a temporary workbench for sawing wood, nailing things together, etc. Instantly, it is seen differently if someone tells you that it is a valuable antique.

- Jokes are reframes - you are guided to think in one frame and then the frame (meaning or context) changes. How many psychologists does it take to change a light bulb? Answer: Only one, and the light bulb must want to change!

- Fairy tales often use reframes to help children see different perspectives or consequences - 'crying wolf'.

- An excuse is a reframe that attributes a different meaning or context to your behaviours.

Some more notable reframes are:

- During the 1984 US presidential campaign, there was considerable concern about Ronald Reagan's age. Speaking during the presidential debate with Walter Mondale, Reagan said 'I will not make age an issue of this campaign. I am not going to exploit, for political purposes, my opponent's youth and inexperience.' Reagan's age was not an issue for the remainder of the campaign!

- There is a story about Thomas Watson Sr., the first President of IBM. A young worker had made a mistake that lost IBM $1 M in business. She was called in to the President's office and as she walked in she said, 'Well, I guess you have called me here to fire me.' 'Fire you?' Mr Watson replied, 'I just spent $1 M on your education!'

- A father brought his headstrong daughter to see Milton Erickson - the famous hypnotherapist. He said to Erickson; 'My daughter doesn't listen to her mother or me. She is always expressing her own opinion.' After the father finished describing his daughter's problem, Erickson replied; 'Now isn't it good that she will be able to stand on her own two feet when she is ready to leave home?' The father sat in stunned silence. That was the extent of the therapy - the father now saw his daughter's behaviour as a useful resource later in her life.

There are two basic forms of reframe - *content* (or meaning) and *context (*or situation*)* reframes.

Content Reframe:

The content or meaning of a situation is influenced by what we choose to focus on. An electrical power failure can be viewed as disruptive and a major personal disaster, given all you have to get done. Or it can be viewed as an opportunity to spend some intimate time with your spouse or to have fun with your children, finding fun ways to enjoy the situation.

A content reframe is useful for statements such as 'I get annoyed when my boss stands behind me while I'm working.' Notice how she has taken the situation and given it a specific meaning - which may or may not be true - and in so doing limits her resourcefulness and possible courses of action. To reframe this situation ask questions such as:

- What other meaning could the boss's behaviour have? For what purpose does he do it? A possible reframe might be: 'Maybe he wants to help and doesn't know how to offer his assistance in any other way?'

- What is the positive value in this behaviour? The positive value could be related to the boss's behaviour (as above) or it could be related to the speaker's behaviour. A possible reframe might be: 'Isn't it great that you know your boundaries and are not prepared to allow someone to violate them?'

Context Reframe:

Almost all our behaviours could be thought of as useful or appropriate in some context. Interrupting a speaker by standing up and offering your view in the middle of her lecture would almost certainly be judged inappropriate. But to do so at the end of the presentation, in order to provide a different perspective, may be welcomed by all present.

A context reframe is therefore useful for statements such as 'I am too pushy' or 'I wish I did not focus on what could go wrong.' In this type of situation, the speaker has assumed that this type of behaviour has no value and is having an impact on their confidence and how they behave. What you can do as a questioner is to help them discover when those behaviours might be of value by getting them to consider the question of when or where would this behaviour be useful or viewed as a resource?' A possible reframe question might be:

'Isn't that a great skill to have when you need to get things done or to avoid potential problems?'

Once you have the other person more feeling better about things, you can then assist him or her to discover behaviours that may be more appropriate in other situations.

Concluding Thoughts

When you start using these very powerful questions you do need to be careful:

- Make sure you have rapport, i.e. you are both on good, friendly and safe terms and have their permission to offer a question like this.

- You may believe your reframe question is the best ever and yet it may not work for the other person. Don't be discouraged: they may simply have a different model of the world from you.

- If you present the reframe in the form of a question or a metaphor (story), it will most likely be more fully considered than if you present it as a statement of fact.

I once heard a great little example. A man was walking along a country road many, many years ago carrying all his belongings. He stopped when he saw a farmer in the field and asked him 'I am thinking of settling down in the next village. How friendly are the people there?' The wise farmer said 'How friendly were the people in the last place you lived?' He replied that they were very unfriendly and that was the reason he left. The farmer then paused and said 'I think you'll find the people in the village ahead much the same as those of the village you left!'

Remember you can't reframe anyone other than yourself because only you live in your world. The best you can do is to ask someone to consider your reframe and then he or she can choose whether or not it reframes their own experience.

How Can Questions Challenge Assumptions?

What Might You Have Learned In This Chapter?

- How do we make assumptions and what impact do they have?
- In what situations might you find you or others making limiting assumptions?
- What is reframing and when is it useful?

Top 10 Questions To Help You To Challenge Assumptions More Effectively

1. What assumptions are we making about this and how certain are we about them?
2. What would make a reasonable person act in this way?
3. If you knew you are good enough, what would you do and how would you feel?
4. If you could make one change in your life, what would it be?
5. If you were not afraid, what would you do?
6. How confident are you about ... on a scale of 1-10? If not 10 what would get you to 10? If ten, what are you assuming that gives you that belief?
7. If you knew the opposite to be true for you, what would you be doing, or what would be happening differently?
8. What would be a freeing assumption for you?
9. I am not sure I understand. Could you please explain it to me further?
10. What has led you to believe that?

How Can Questions Develop Momentum?

> Even if you are on the right track, you will get run over if you just sit there.
>
> **Will Rogers**

Moving from good intention to action and building momentum is always one of the most difficult things to achieve. Why? Because of the inertia that accompanies the current ways of doing things. To do something new means giving up doing something you are doing right now or finding additional energy or resources from somewhere else.

It also means moving from the known, safe and comfortable into the unknown, which always feels more risky and difficult.

I find people are often limited in what they believe they can achieve by what's happened in the past. While learning lessons from the past can guide you, it shouldn't bind you. People can get extremely negative and de-motivated. The trick is to re-frame their thinking, to adopt new perspectives and to have the confidence to take the first few steps.

Consider this for a moment. Write your name with the hand you least favour. Everyone can do it … eventually. But what did you have to do to do it? You had to focus and concentrate. Writing your name with your usual hand is easy – you don't really have to think what you are doing. It's the same for moving into new action. Think of these as being 'left-handed' (excuse me if you are naturally left-handed). Normal activity is right-handed.

Now, of course, you can always tell people what to do and follow up rigorously to make sure they do it. This will work – but only to a limited extent. Real change happens when people make positive choices for themselves and develop their own thinking and capability to do the task. Good questioning is the only way to ignite other peoples' thinking.

Good questions in this area can focus people, get them thinking about how exciting it will be to achieve their desired outcomes, address limiting beliefs, overcome hurdles, and (very importantly) challenge old and probably non-useful habits and build new, more useful ones.

One of the problems can often be a desire to be perfect, or at least reasonably good, at something before we will even attempt it. But, of course, we can never acquire experience unless we try. And so we go around this endless circuit and end up being perfectly wrong instead of reasonably right.

I remember, many years ago, a great example of this. I was attending a conference in Germany and was met at the airport by the conference organiser. She greeted me in several languages. I asked her how many languages she spoke. She replied seven fluently and a few others ok. I said that, being British, we are very lazy at languages because everyone else likes to practice their English with us. I admitted that I was able to speak only English. She then said 'Can you say "hello" in German?' I replied with 'Guten Morgen'. She said 'So you *can* speak German!'

I puzzled for a while, wondering what she had meant. Then I realised that she was questioning how many words of any language you need to know in order to say that you can speak that language. For example, although I am a native English speaker there are still many English words I don't know. The fact that I have only a smattering of German stopped me from trying - and if I never try I will never learn German.

Great Implementation Questions

How can we ensure we get started and build momentum?

Whatever you can do, or dream you can, begin it. Boldness has genius, power, and magic in it. Begin it now ...

Goethe

Business ideas are great but they are not much good unless you implement them. That is the hardest part because this takes you into new territory, outside of your comfort zones. You and others will need persuasion and motivation. Obstructions will need to be overcome. Where will you get the energy for action? The following are some specific areas to address and questions to use to help you get your ideas into action.

Dissatisfaction can often be the 'prod' you need to spot potential problems and opportunities.

- What is it that you are dissatisfied with that is pushing you to take action?

- What could you do to make that source of dissatisfaction more obvious to you?

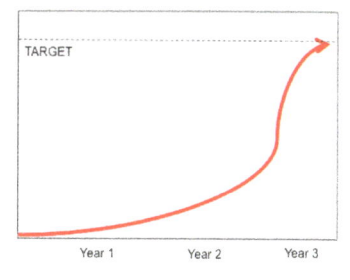

A way of moving people into action to achieve a long term goal is to introduce a sense of urgency and dissatisfaction into where they are in their progress towards achieving this goal. Often if the goal is (say) three years away, there is a tendency for those involved to leave things until later and hope that somehow a miracle will happen in the final year. It's often what's called the 'hockey stick' phenomenon.

How Can Questions Develop Momentum?

A way of getting round this is by planning 'back from the future'. In this process you ask questions as follows:

1. Where would we need to be at the end of year 2 if we are going to be confident of achieving our target at the end of year 3?

then ask

2. Where would we need to be at the end of year 1 if we are going to be confident of achieving our target at the end of year 2?

When you do this, those involved suddenly appreciate the scale of what needs to be achieved in year one and they realise the graph looks more like the one shown on the left. It's a very different type of hockey stick!

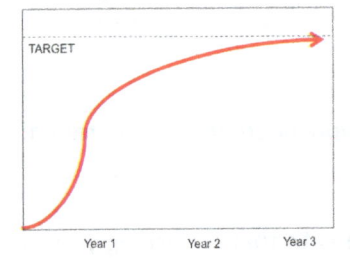

Often an obstruction will be **lack of clarity** regarding what you or they need to do. Being absolutely clear on your plans and how you are going to achieve them can be the difference that makes the difference. Personally I have always found my motivation improves dramatically when I can see a clear cause and effect link between the things I am currently doing and the results I am hoping to achieve.

- What is your objective and can you state it in a sentence or two?

- Can you draw a picture of it?

- Can you make a map of where you need to go and the things you need to do?

- What planning do you need to do?

- Can you visualise reaching your objective?

Take the first step. You either let your life slip away by not doing the things you want to do, or you get up and do them. Many of our goals are left stranded on a little island called 'Someday I might'. We can't wait for things to happen - you can't score a goal if you're not on the field. Momentum is a huge thing, and to get momentum you have to start. We may be watching a football game. One team is losing 3-0. The losing team scores a goal – nothing to worry about thinks the winning team. They score another goal and the whole dynamic changes

- What three things can you do **now** to reach your goals?
- For each of these, what's the smallest thing you can do today that will create momentum into tomorrow?

Get rid of excuses. It often takes more energy to get rid of excuses than it did to come up with the opportunity in the first place. Go back to the chapter on assumptions and ask questions that will help you recognise whether your excuses are just that or real issues to be addressed

According to some, Hernando Cortez set sail on the final leg of his voyage from Cuba to Mexico in February 1519. His plan was simple. Go to Mexico, conquer it and become rich and famous. When he and his men arrived on the shores of Yucatan, they received news that the forces against them and difficulties they would face were larger and far greater than they had been led to believe. The men became nervous, unsettled and talked of going home. That night Cortez, obviously a very single-minded and driven man, was supposed to have taken some of his most trusted men out in a rowing boat and set fire to their own ships. This meant that Cortez and his army would either conquer and return alive on somebody else's boats, or that they would have to die trying.

Hence the expression, 'burning your boats'

- What three factors will make it difficult to achieve your objectives?

- How could you burn your boats?

Try to have something at stake. This could be anything from survival, self-esteem, money or reputation so that you'll be motivated to make your idea successful. It is always interesting to see how organisations can sometimes be galvanised by the need to survive. In our current economic recession I have noticed companies doing things that they should have done in better times, but it was harder to make that decision when nothing appeared to be at stake.

One idea is to tell as many people as possible of your plans; it makes it embarrassing for you not to follow them through. This certainly works for me. I have made big personal changes like getting fit and losing weight, when I set myself a challenge like running a half marathon and getting people to sponsor me. How about wagering something worthwhile on the outcome?

- What have you got or could you have at stake?

Create a support system. It's much easier to be successful if you create an environment that expects you to succeed and will support you in doing so. This is the more positive version of the previous point. Whenever I have implemented change in the past it's often been due to the support of friends, colleagues and family. Writing this book has been a great example of this.

- Who could be part of your support system and how can you engage them?

It's no good unless it sells. You can have the greatest idea in the world, but if you can't sell it you won't get very far.

- List three reasons why someone would buy your idea, or product or service?

- What are the benefits for them?

- How could you make it more attractive to them?

Be courageous.

I learned that courage was not the absence of fear, but the triumph over it. The brave man is not he who does not feel afraid, but he who conquers that fear'

Nelson Mandela

- What gives you the courage to act on your ideas?

Set yourself a deadline. We all tend to work better to a deadline: it's when you have to do what has to be done.

- What tight deadlines can you give yourself?

Fight for it. Change is inevitable and people tend to resist change. Much of the world has its defences up to keep out new ideas. You need to become a warrior and do what's necessary to make your idea a reality.

Try? There is no try. There is only do or not do.

Yoda

If you hear yourself, or anyone else, say they are going to try, recognise that it probably isn't going to happen. Ask yourself, or others, not when they are going to try but when they are going to *do*.

- What resistance do you expect to your idea and how can you overcome it?

- What are you willing to do to put your ideas into action?

Being persistent. Behind every success there is usually a story of dogged determination to convince other people of a good idea. One of the great examples of this was Abraham Lincoln. He failed in business in 1831. He was defeated for state legislator in 1832. He tried another business in 1833. It failed. His fiancée died in 1835. He had a nervous breakdown in 1836. In 1843 he ran for Congress and was defeated. He tried again in 1848 and was defeated again. He tried running for the Senate in 1855. He lost. The next year he ran for Vice-President and lost. In 1859 he ran for the Senate again and was defeated. In 1860, the man who signed his name A. Lincoln was elected the 16th President of the United States. The difference between history's boldest accomplishments and its most staggering failures is often, simply, the diligent will to persevere.

Press on. Nothing in the world can take the place of persistence. Talent will not: nothing is more common than unsuccessful men with talent. Genius will not: un-rewarded genius is almost a proverb. Education alone will not: the world is full of educated derelicts. Persistence and determination alone are omnipotent

Calvin Coolidge

- How persistent are you?

Is this a time of action? Many of us have achieved success in our careers by being action orientated and decisive. Many times this is the right way to be, but being decisive does not necessarily mean making decisions instantly. The best decisions are the ones made when they have to be or should be made. Making decisions quickly, just for the sake of it, can prove ineffective and costly. If the time is available before a decision has to be made then its best to use it to reflect. Just reflecting on the possible decision will allow others to buy in, allow time for critical events to unfold, and allow time to generate more options.

Asking 'Is this a time for action?' allows you or others to stop and consider whether this is indeed the most propitious time. Good decision making and problem solving usually comes from a combination of creatively generating options (so at least you have other options to compare against the solution you had in mind!) and logically prioritising to choose the best option.

Given time constraints, the problem is how do we make sure we spend the right amount of time on option generation and closing down and ensure we get into the action zone? This is where this question is so powerful. If a decision doesn't have to be made now ask:

- When is the best time to make this decision?

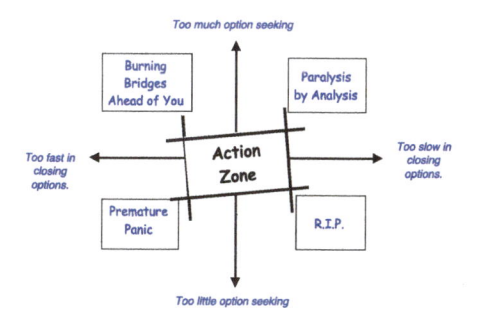

This diagram can also be a useful one to share with your team to make sure they are considering this question carefully. It enables the team to examine their decision making carefully and ask questions around whether they are falling into any of the traps illustrated in the diagram.

Finally another excellent question is:

- What do you need to do to make sure that you don't succeed here?

The unexpectedness and daring of this question usually make people laugh, but there is also a valuable lesson in it too! What I have typically found is that when we look at the list we generate as a result of asking this question, quite a few of the actions listed had a fair chance of actually happening!

What Might You Have Learned In This Chapter?

- What stops us from taking action?
- What is the importance of momentum?
- What are some of the blocks that stop us taking action?

Top 10 Questions To Help You To Challenge Assumptions More Effectively

1. What three things can you do **now** to reach your goals?
2. For each of these, what's smallest thing you can do today that will create momentum into tomorrow?
3. If our success was completely guaranteed, what bold steps might we choose?
4. What are you willing to do to put your ideas into action?
5. List three reasons why someone would buy your idea, product or service?
6. What tight deadlines can you give yourself?
7. What gives you the courage to act on your ideas?
8. Who could be part of your support system and how can you engage them?
9. What have you got or could you have at stake?
10. How could you burn your boats?

How Can Questions Unleash Creativity?

Sometimes we stare so long at a door that is closing that we see too late the one that is open.

Alexander Graham Bell

What Makes Creativity Important?

If change is a condition of business existence, where do the new ideas come from? Almost any technological or product advance can be copied in a couple of months - so where does an organisation's competitive advantage live? The answer to both these questions seems to be 'people'. You can't innovate by committee.

Individual managers and companies these days are almost trained to be risk-averse. This is especially true when times are hard. Managers emphasise command and control because the risks of getting things wrong are too great. Creative ideas are by their very nature difficult to manage and can be seen as dangerous.

There's also a hierarchical effect. Coming up with the ideas is sometimes seen as the province of senior managers - who may be much better at controlling, rather than being creative.

Rational planning can create a good, efficient organisation. But, combined with new IT systems, it tends to make all companies look and act alike. Creativity is individual. Only creativity can provide the transforming idea that makes a good organisation a great one and leaves others trying to catch up. Creativity is human, and businesses are having to adopt a more human tone of voice, either because that's what their customers expect or because it differentiates organisations.

So, if creativity is so important, how can we use questions to help create it and to prise people from their risk-averse shells? In this chapter we will look at this in detail

If we had to double our performance in the same timescale what would we do differently?

People's initial reaction to this question is that it would be impossible. But stick with it. Ask them to live in this impossible world for just ten minutes and brainstorm ideas about how to achieve this apparently impossible goal. When they have done this, ask if any of the ideas they have generated might still be applicable when we return to the 'real' world. Inevitably they will surprise themselves, as many of the ideas they brainstormed for the 'impossible' goal are still very much valid in the 'real' world!

Why is this? It's all about the baggage we carry with us. Incremental thinking allows us to take this baggage with us while step change thinking does not.

If I were to ask you how you could increase the height over which you could jump by 3-6 inches, what would your answers be? I expect they would include getting fitter, having coaching on technique or taking a longer run up.

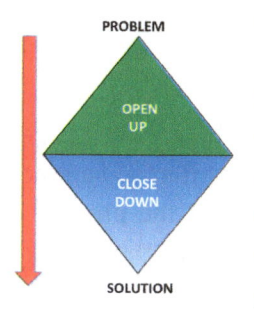

But what if I were to ask you to get over an eight-foot hurdle? Immediately you have to think far more creatively and come up with suggestions such as adding springs to your feet, using a ladder, or doing a pole vault. You are not even able to consider merely doing a little more of what you already know. It is an entirely new group of ideas and different thinking.

It is all too easy to get trapped by current ways of doing things. Asking people to do just a little bit more can often cause stress because they often think they are doing as well as they can now. They need to break out of the current mind set and consider new possibilities. In doing so you will see how energised they can become.

I have found that creativity is present in everybody. Undoubtedly some of us are more creative than others, but I have found when working with many, many, teams over the last 30 years that, given the right circumstances, even those who think themselves lacking in creativity can become full of ideas.

Since the late nineteenth century, when Herman Helmholtz began the quest, many great thinkers have been trying to classify the successive steps in the creative problem-solving process. All have produced models, some having named more steps than others.

The simplest way to look at it is to consider this diagram. Any decision making or problem solving process must involve an opening up or creative stage and a closing down or choosing stage. The opening up stage is vital. If we only have one option to choose from how can we possibly know it's the best one if we have nothing to compare it with?

So the opening up stage is the creative one. It is especially important for important decisions or when you are facing a problem or issue that keeps arising. If you keep on doing what you have always done you will get what you have always got - or worse.

Introducing people to this model, especially those who are keen to get decisions made and to take action, helps them realise that you are not just entering a flight of fancy but that this is part of the process is necessary in order to get to the best decision. This helps them relax - an important part of the creative process as we have seen.

We have to create the right circumstances and the first of these is that there must be an issue to overcome. Very few people can be creative unless they are focussing on some issue. In Japan they call this process 'forced creativity' and the more challenging the problem to be overcome or gaol to be achieved, the more likely it is that people will come up with new and different ideas.

Initially, what can work here is to go back to our questions on goals and outcomes. So what questions might work here?

Having determined a powerful goal or outcome, you can easily play around with it as shown at the beginning of the chapter. By asking questions that remove people from their current reality, we can eliminate the tendency towards incremental thinking. A word of caution: it can be hard for people simply to accept doubling the goal, for example, unless you say to them that we are going to step out of their real world for a short period of time.

While it is important to set people a challenging goal, it's important to get this just right. Stress and creativity are not good bedfellows. People need to be in the creative mood. In order to demonstrate this, try and solve this test.

(By the way, it has been shown that it can be done by a 12-year-old child with average intelligence in twenty seconds. So the question for you is: 'How much faster can you do it?')

- I like Puccini less than Verdi
- I dislike Wagner less than Britten
- I don't enjoy Donizetti as much as Puccini
- Which composer do I like least?

How Can Questions Unleash Creativity?

The question is how did it help knowing that it could be solved by a 12 year old in twenty seconds? Not much I guess. In fact in takes an average twelve-year old over five minutes to solve it. Feeling better?

You need to get people into a relaxed and playful mood for them to be truly creative. In the ego state model referred to in the chapter on assertiveness, it's the child-like ego state that is a good one to adopt for this purpose. It seems that pictures, sounds, stories, etc., all help to create this mood.

If we knew what we were doing, it would not be called research would it?

Albert Einstein

Even when you have helped them set a challenging goal you may still find that people need to become more creative, especially when they may have limiting assumptions about what is possible. The focus of our questions now is to unlock typical mental blocks. These may include:

- The Right Answer
- That's Not Logical
- Follow the Rules
- Be Practical
- Play Is Frivolous
- That's Not My Area
- Avoid Ambiguity
- Don't Be Foolish

- To Err Is Wrong

- I'm Not Creative

To open these blocks, be aware of them - and then temporarily forget them.

A person needs a little madness, or else they never dare cut the rope and be free.

Nikos Kazantzakis

Another way to get people into the creative mode is by use of metaphors. Ask people to make a metaphor of the problem you are currently dealing with, or a concept you're developing. Then ask them to simply compare the concept with the metaphor and see what similarities exist. Basically you are asking them to use one idea to highlight another. See how this works by using some of these metaphors. Ask people how an idea compares with:

- Running for office
- Running a marathon
- Riding a roller coaster
- Courting a woman
- Fighting a disease
- Sailing a ship in rough seas
- Attending a church service
- Performing a magic trick

- Cooking a fancy meal
- Starting a revolution
- Prospecting for gold
- Putting out a fire
- Running a day care centre
- Doing stand-up comedy
- Going on a diet
- Colonising a territory

- Building a house
- Negotiating a contract
- Planting a garden
- Getting a divorce
- Pruning a tree
- Spreading propaganda
- Going fishing
- Having a baby
- Arranging flowers
- Learning a new language

I have found that by using simple questions around metaphors I can create a lot of fun but also some genuinely creative ideas. And all you have done is ask a few questions. Below are some examples that participants have come up with in creative warm-up exercises:

Life is like a banana. You start out all green and get soft and mushy with age. Some people want to be one of the bunch, while others want to be top banana. You have to take care not to slip on the externals. And finally, you have to strip off the outer coating to get to the fruit.

Life is like riding a lift. It has lots of ups and downs and someone is always pushing your buttons. Sometimes you get the shaft, but what really bothers you are the jerks.

Similar to the metaphor process is the technique of getting people to view an issue from a different perspective. For example, what if someone else was trying to solve your problem? A client of mine was trying to launch a new and exciting product but needed the support and partnership of a key manufacturer. They were finding it difficult to make progress. I simply asked what would someone like Richard Branson do if faced with this issue? They thought for a while and responded 'Get on the next plane to Japan and sit outside the CEO's office until he was prepared to talk to us.' Guess what, they did just that and, guess what, they got their partnership.

So try some of these the next time you want someone to think differently without giving them the answer. What would happen if one of the following were trying to solve this problem:

- Winston Churchill
- Mother Theresa
- The Godfather
- Sigmund Freud
- Jesus
- Wonder Woman
- A 7 Year Old Child

You can ask some further question to help them explore their thinking, such as:

- What assumptions would they bring?
- What special twists would they give to it?
- What innovative changes would they make?
- What special expertise would they bring?

Sometimes it's better to ask them to think about someone they admire rather than naming a person or character. This allows them ownership.

Another creative process I have used is to ask someone 'What if you were the problem?' It sounds strange, but bear with me. Suppose you were trying to redesign a toaster, for example. You could ask:

How Can Questions Unleash Creativity?

- What would it be like to be a toaster?
    - How would you receive the bread?
    - What would it be like when your heating elements go?
    - What happens when then crumbs fall to the bottom?

Or maybe you were trying to redesign a Formula One engine:

- What would it be like to be an F1 engine?
    - How would it feel to be revved up fast?
    - How would you like being thrown around corners?
    - What does it feel like when you are getting overheated?

When people are really warmed up to be creative, I have found random challenge questions to be really effective in encouraging them to think differently. The process works like this. When you or someone you are working with is stuck as to what to do next, select something from the world at random. For example:

- Pick the sixth word on page 276 of your dictionary.
- Open a magazine, count until you reach the 11th advert -what is it?
- Open the shares page of the newspaper. Pick the company 13th down on the third column. What product does it make?

Then ask 'How does this random thing apply to your situation?' Suggest they take their time as somewhere there will a connection and it is their job to find it.

An example. There is a graffiti problem in our town. By random selection you come up with the word bikini. This leads to the suggestion that if the wall was more attractive perhaps people would not deface it.

Once you and the people around you have got used to asking questions like this, try using magic. Ask them to imagine a magic substance, which could do anything you told it to. For example, what if we had some magic to:

- Mark the cars that jump lights?
- Take care of routine shopping?
- Create a person who wants to be a permanent number two?
- Create a situation where everyone is working together towards a common solution?

What would that magic substance look like? Again get people to work at this, as the answer might not be immediate

Working backwards is a useful process when the gap to bridge seems too wide. Invite people to create what are called 'intermediate islands' so the process would work something like this:

- How do we get to A?
- If we could get to B we could get to A
- If we could get to C we could get to B and so on

For example: If shoplifters could easily be caught they would keep away. How can we demonstrate to shoplifters that they will be caught? We could use video cameras.

How Can Questions Unleash Creativity?

There are many, many ways of encouraging people to be creative. What would happen if you played around and tried some?

The final one I will leave you with is simply to ask 'What if?' and then finish the question with some contrary-to-fact condition, idea or situation.

- What if animals were more intelligent than people?
- What if men also had babies?
- What if we could make music by playing vegetables?
- What if people had to marry people who were 20 years younger or older than themselves?
- What if people had to spend at least a third of the year living outside the country where they were born?
- What if we lived life backwards?

Finally, one of my favourites has always been 'What would we do if we really wanted to mess this up?' I have found this to be a wonderful question to ask when you and your team have, for example, developed a project plan or planned an event. It creates a lot of high-energy fun followed by a realisation that many of the things we have come up with could very well happen and we need to ensure that they don't!

So, I hope I have convinced you (if you were not already convinced) of the value of creativity and how once again by posing simple questions you can encourage yourself and others to become more creative.

What Might You Have Learned In This Chapter?

- What makes creativity even more important today?
- When is the right time to be creative?
- What kinds of questions stimulate creativity?

My Top 10 Questions To Help You To Become More Creative

1. What have you done differently today?
2. What if someone famous was trying to solve this problem?
3. What would we do if we really tried to mess this up?
4. What would happen if we had to double performance?
5. In what ways is implementing this project like starting a revolution?
6. What if we lived life backwards?
7. What can I do to step outside my comfort zone today?
8. How will our industry still be relevant in the year 2020?
9. What's interesting about that idea?
10. What would happen if ...?

How Can Questions Accelerate Learning?

'Insanity: doing the same thing over and over again and expecting different results'.

Albert Einstein

The fascinating science of neuroscience – how the brain actually works - is telling us more and more about how we learn and how we form memories. Using the latest electronic equipment and scanners they are able to see, in real time, which parts of the brain light up when different things are happening

These advances have confirmed what we all guessed: that we learn most when we have a chance to test and discuss our ideas with other people we trust. We also only store memories if we have had a chance to stand back and reflect and link new information to previously stored memories

One of the biggest challenges for us in this busy, distracting world is how we turn short-term memory and processing into longer-term memory.

Most of us have crammed for exams from time to time. This will work for a short time but most of these facts and figures are soon lost as soon as the exams are over unless we have transferred them into longer-term memory

A number of lessons about learning have been drawn from this field of science:

- As we get older, our brains are more plastic than we once thought and we can still store lots of new memories. However, it seems that in order to achieve this we don't so much lay down new memories but rather recall old ones, test and then reshape them with new information, and then store them again. This has significant implications on how we help people through the learning process

- It seems we are social learners. We are pre-programmed to learn with and from other people. It's when we are in social groups that we test our ideas and after testing build them into our longer memories. Without this process, ideas and thoughts tend not to find a true home in our long-term memories. This has implications for how we ask questions to capture learning in teams.

- Thirdly, we don't learn only facts and data. We associate that information with every element of the context at the time. For example, we might remember our teacher as well as what she taught us. Specifically, we tend to store information more robustly if there is a strong emotion associated with it. That's why, for instance, most of us can remember what we were doing on 9/11 but few of us can remember what we were doing the day before. Again this suggests people will learn better when they are strongly motivated. Questions can play a key role in discovering or creating that motivation.

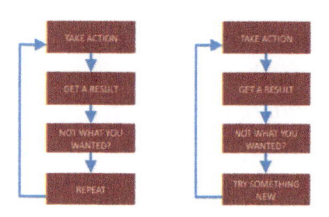

I was lucky enough a number of years ago to visit best practice companies around the world. I believed then, and still believe, that the Japanese are the best at manufacturing. On one memorable visit to a car plant one of the CEOs who was in my party asked why they were so open about showing what they did. 'Aren't you afraid we might copy you?' The response, which perhaps seemed slightly arrogant but was certainly true at the time, was: 'We hope that's what you do. It's not copying that is the key to success, it's the learning process itself. By the time you have wasted time trying to copy without the learning behind it we will have moved further ahead!'

The lesson here is clear: if we are to learn from success and failure we need to invest time and discuss what has happened with our colleagues in an environment free from blame. This does not mean that holding people accountable for achieving results is not important. It's *how* we hold people to account for maintaining a high standard and then how we discuss with them what we have learned from taking action.

> *I have learned from my mistakes, and I am sure I can repeat them exactly.*
>
> **Peter Cook**

Be honest, how often do you and your team review what has gone on and spend time learning the lessons? In my experience, I don't find this a common practice. There can be several reasons for this. One is the sheer pace of life and change. The second is the 'If it's gone well let's not dig too deeply...' syndrome, '... as we may find some not so good stuff and we get little recognition anyway!' Thirdly, it's often because we are not sure if it's been a success or not as plans and goals were vague in the first place. In this regard I always like the little epigram about Columbus:

> *When he set out he didn't know where he was going.*
>
> *When he got there he didn't know where he was.*
>
> *When he got back he didn't know where he had been.*
>
> *And he did it all on borrowed finance'*

Finally if it's gone badly it's often about finding who to blame. Very few find that a comfortable process and try to hide things or put a smoke screen around the unpalatable bits

As with many things we have discussed so far in this book, the solution is not a clever technique. It's rather about doing what we do with a different mind-set. In this case it's about:

- Investing time in reviewing and reflecting with those involved

- Conducting the review in a 'safe' way so that everyone can be honest

- Still holding people to a high standard

If we have set clear goals and clear measures then we have a sound foundation. I have always liked the Plan-Do-Check-Act or Plan-Do-Check-Adjust (PDCA) model. It's a four-step model used extensively in best practice companies.

This model can seem simple and even simplistic. But the fact is that many organisations fail to follow through the stages of this process, especially the check and act stages.

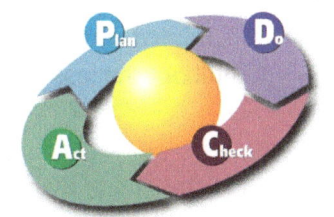

Often the single difference between organisations that are successful and those who are less so, is whether they follow this process through on a regular basis or not. The typical problem you will see in less successful organisations and initiatives, is that a plan is put in place and then not checked and learned from. As a result the search goes on to try something new rather that learning and making it work

The steps in each successive PDCA cycle are:

PLAN In this step you establish the objectives and timescales and then the processes and resources necessary to deliver results in accordance with the expected output (the target or goals).

DO During this step you implement the plan, execute the process, make the product or deliver the service. You also collect data for measuring and analysis in the following CHECK and ACT steps.

CHECK Now the team studies the actual results (measured and collected in DO above) and compares them against the expected results (targets or goals from the PLAN) to find any differences. You look for deviation in implementation from the plan and also look for the appropriateness/completeness of the plan to enable the execution, i.e. DO. This is the key sage of learning and reflection.

ACT As a result of the lessons learned from the CHECK stage, you can now agree and implement any corrective actions on significant differences between actual and planned results.

All the stages are essential, but the ones that are missed out most often are the CHECK and ACT stages. Even if we do pull out the lessons we don't always apply them.

The key way of addressing this is to build in checks at the end of every project, on a regular (say) monthly basis, when tracking progress against goals, and then more extensively at year end so that lessons can be built into next year's plans. Again the relatively simple way of making this happen is to plan these in the diary.

I sometimes take leaders on my programmes away for a weekend on a sailing boat at sea. They have tasks to do and they are in control of the boat. I am there to observe, provide technical guidance and make sure they don't do anything that is dangerous. One of the key lessons they draw from this back in the workplace is the idea of meeting regularly (often daily) as a team to check everyone is clear about their responsibilities, to resolve any potential issues and to acknowledge lessons learned. In work generally they say it's easy not to do this especially in a climate of vague non-stretching goals.

> Controlling your destiny requires two things: a reasonable understanding of how the competitive world is evolving, and a profound understanding of the cause and effect relationship between the things you do and the results that are achieved

> **John Fly - Milliken & Co**

At these reviews you ask your team how well they have progressed against goals and objectives. The objectives, which are measurable, are used as indicators to check progress - not sticks to whack people with. If they are ahead or behind plan they are asked what has helped or hindered them and what have they learned. For every conclusion they are asked to show how they know this. They must have data to support their conclusions. You should use what are called process questions rather than ones focused purely on end results. For example:

- What has helped or hindered progress?
- How do you know?
- What will you do differently from now on?
- What have you learned that will help in the future?
- How will this affect your expected results for the next period?
- If results are not as good as planned, is there anything else that could be done?
- What could anyone else do to help?
- How can we build these lessons into future plans and actions?

As a result of the review you then build in any changes into the plan for the next month. In this way everybody learns and improves. The focus is on improvement aligned to goals. This process I call **'Triple Vision'**. It means focusing on:

- The overall goal in sight. This means setting high standards while chunking the goal up into manageable bite-sized bits. The overall goal is motivational - the 'chunks' give you the belief that you can do it.

- What you are doing now. Focussing on the future while you are undertaking a project now can lead to distraction and uncertainty, which will affect performance now. Arnold Schwarzenegger has said of his training that doing an exercise movement once with awareness was worth ten times an exercise done while distracted.

- Recognising progress made. Self to self-comparisons are far more positive and effective than self to other comparisons as many successful athletes will testify. Comparing against others means you are supposed to feel good if you come out better and bad if you don't. Self to self will always bring out the positive lessons.

All that I have talked about is clearly relevant to the questions you need to ask to generate real learning.

- Real learning takes place when new information can be connected to past experiences and learning.

- It happens more effectively when people are in groups.

- It only happens when you invest time in a safe way to allow real reflection.

What Might You Have Learned In This Chapter About Using Questions To Promote Learning?

- How important is it to focus on learning?

- What do we need to do to ensure we reflect on lessons learned?

- When was the last time you invested time in real learning?

Top 10 Questions To Help You To Promote Learning

1. What do you already know that might have relevance here?

2. What have we achieved so far?

3. What has helped or hindered progress?

4. What specifically was the difference that made the difference this time?

5. What have we learned from this experience and how will we use that knowledge?

6. How important is applying what you have learned in the future?

7. How have you made a difference today?

8. How has this experience helped in achieving our goal?

9. What do you notice when things are going well?

10. What do we need to do to get back on track?

How Can Questions Increase Assertiveness?

In this chapter we will look at what assertiveness is all about and why it's important. Understanding what it is, and how we get into situations when we are less assertive that we should be, helps us understand what we can do about it.

My proposition is that it takes a lot of emotional energy and even courage to stand up for yourself and argue your corner in the face of someone who is being aggressive or patronising and who is certainly not allowing you the space to put forward your views

However, if we understand these situations better we can allow great questions to do the work for us. This requires far less emotional energy and at the same time will bring you greater success.

What is assertiveness?

Assertiveness is being able to stand up for yourself, making sure your opinions and feelings are considered and not letting other people always get their way. It is not the same as aggressiveness. You can be assertive without being forceful or rude. Instead, it is stating clearly what you expect and insisting that your rights are considered.

Assertion is a skill that can be learnt. It is a way of communicating and behaving with others that helps the person to become more confident and aware of themselves.

At some time in our lives, however confident we are, we will find it difficult to deal with certain situations we encounter. Examples of these could be:

- Speaking to our boss.

- Asking someone to return something they have borrowed.

- Dealing with difficult people.

- Communicating our feelings to our friends, family or partner.

Often in life we deal with these situations by losing our temper, by saying nothing or by giving in. This may leave us feeling unhappy, angry, frustrated and out of control - and still may not actually solve the problem. This tendency to react in either an unassertive or an aggressive way may become even more of a problem if we become depressed. The loss of confidence and self-worth that is common in depression may make the person more likely either to give in to everyone around them or, alternatively, to become very irritable towards them. Both responses are unhelpful because they are likely to worsen how you feel (by being frustrated with yourself and others) and add to your problems.

Where does assertiveness come from?

As we grow up we learn to adapt our behaviour as a result of the things that happen to us. We model ourselves on those around us: on our parents, teachers and friends, for example, and on other influences such as television and magazines. If during this time our self-confidence is eroded, perhaps through being bullied or ridiculed at school or criticised within the family, then in our adult lives we may be more likely to react passively or aggressively in similar situations.

Even though someone may have learned to react passively or aggressively in life, they are able to change and learn to become more assertive. We will now look at the effects of acting in an *aggressive* or a *passive* way and then contrast this with the impact of *assertion*.

What is passive behaviour?

Passive behaviour is an inability adequately to express your feelings, needs, rights and opinions. Instead, you exhibit a disproportionate consideration for other's feelings, needs, rights and opinions - as illustrated below:

Feelings: Bottling up your own feelings or expressing them in indirect or unhelpful ways.

Needs: Regarding the other person's needs as more important than your own. Giving in to them all the time.

Rights: The other person has rights but you do not acknowledge your own.

Opinions: You see yourself as having little or nothing to contribute and the other person as always being right. You may be frightened to say what you think in case your beliefs are ridiculed.

The aim of passive behaviour is to avoid conflict at all times and to please others.

What are the effects of passive behaviour?

On you: short-term:

- Reduction of anxiety.
- Avoidance of guilt.
- Martyrdom.

On you: long-term:

- Continuing loss of self-esteem.

- Increased internal tensions leading to stress, anger and growing depression.

There may be *immediate* positive effects of being passive, but the longer lasting effects may be detrimental to your own health and cause others to become increasingly irritated by you and to develop a lack of respect for you.

What does aggressive behaviour look like?

Aggression is very different from assertion. Aggression is expressing your own feelings, needs, rights and opinions with no respect for other people's feelings, needs, rights and opinions - as illustrated below:

Feelings: Expressing your feelings in a demanding, angry and inappropriate way.

Needs: Your own needs are seen as being more important than others' and theirs are ignored or dismissed.

Rights: Standing up for your own rights, but doing so in such a way that you violate the rights of other people.

Opinions: You see yourself as having something to contribute and see other people as having little or nothing to contribute.

The aim of aggression is to win - if necessary at the expense of others. Try to think of a time when someone else has been aggressive to you and ignored your opinions. How did it make you feel about them and yourself?

What are the effects of aggression?

Aggression has both short-term and long-term consequences.

Short-term:

- Release of tension
- The person feels more powerful.

Long-term

- Feelings of guilt and shame.
- Transfers responsibility for anger onto others.
- Decreasing self-confidence and self-esteem.
- Resentment felt by those around the aggressive person.

The short-term effects of aggression may seem rewarding in that you can feel a release because you have got something off your chest. But the longer lasting effects are likely to be far less positive. You can often feel guilty or even ashamed at your outburst which may cause problems for the person addressed and others around you.

Speak when you are angry and you will make the best speech you will ever regret.

Ambrose Bierce

What does assertive behaviour look like?

In contrast to being aggressive or passive, being assertive is expressing your own feelings, needs, rights and opinions while at the same time maintaining respect for other people's feelings, needs, rights and opinions.

Feelings: You are able to express your feelings in a direct, honest and appropriate way.

Needs: You have needs that have to be met, otherwise you feel undervalued, rejected, angry or sad.

Rights: You have basic human rights and it is possible to stand up for your own rights in such a way that you do not violate another person's.

Opinions: You have something to contribute, irrespective of other people's views.

Being assertive is not about winning, it is about being able to walk away feeling that you put across what you wanted to say. Try to think about a time when someone else has been assertive with you and respected your opinion. How did you feel about them and yourself?

About me - I felt: (write here)

About them - I felt: (write here):

What are the benefits of being assertive?

Assertiveness is an **attitude** directed towards both yourself and others in a way that is helpful and honest. When you are being assertive you ask for what you want:

- Directly and openly.

- Appropriately, respecting your own opinions and rights and expecting others to do the same. It's about doing this with confidence and not feeling anxious.

You do not:

- Violate other people's rights.
- Expect other people to magically know what you want.
- Freeze with anxiety and avoid difficult issues.

The result is firstly improved self-confidence. Secondly, you earn mutual respect from others.

Do you have the right to be assertive?

All people have basic human rights that give us dignity as individuals. By not allowing your rights to be violated you are not being selfish but are maintaining your self-respect. As well as being aware of your own rights, if you respect those of other people you have the foundation for assertive communication.

There are no real rules for this but the following list is generally accepted as describing what assertiveness looks like in practice and what your 'rights' are.

I have the right to:

1. Respect myself - who I am and what I do.
2. Recognise my own needs as an individual - that is separate from what is expected of me in particular roles, such as, *son, daughter, brother, sister, employee.*

3. Make clear 'I' statements about how I feel and what I think. For example, '*I feel very uncomfortable with your decision*'.

4. Allow myself to make mistakes, recognising that it is normal to make mistakes.

5. Change my mind should I choose.

6. Ask for 'thinking it over' time. For example, when people ask you to do something, you have the right to say '*I would like to think it over and I will let you know my decision by the end of the week*'.

7. Allow myself to enjoy my successes - that is by being pleased with what I have done and sharing it with others.

8. Asking for what I want, rather than hoping someone will notice what I want.

9. Recognise that I am not responsible for the behaviour of other adults.

10. Respect other people and their right to be assertive and expect the same in return

It's one thing to acknowledge these rights. It's quite another to be honest with yourself and ask to what extent do you believe them and actually put them into practice? So, below is a questionnaire to allow you to do this and then to reflect on the results.

Currently, do you believe each of these rules and apply them?

How Can Questions Increase Assertiveness?

	Do I believe this rule to be true?		Have I applied it in the last week?	
	Yes	No	Yes	No
Respect myself - who I am and what I do.				
Recognise my own needs as an individual - separate from particular roles				
Make clear 'I' statements about how I feel and what I think.				
Allow myself to make mistakes, recognising that this is normal.				
Change my mind, should I choose.				
Ask for 'thinking it over' time.				
Allow myself to enjoy my successes.				
Ask for what I want, rather than hoping someone will notice what I want.				
Recognise that I am not responsible for the behaviour of other adults.				
Respect other people and their right to be assertive and expect the same in return.				

Most of us will identify areas where we need to improve, become more assertive and allow others to do the same. As we will see, using questions can allow you to apply these 'rules' without becoming aggressive.

However, before we do this let's look at another bit of theory that has some very practical implications, both in terms of being more assertive and also regarding the type of questions we might ask to help us do so. This theory is called Transactional Analysis or TA for short.

Transactional Analysis is one of the most accessible theories of modern psychology. TA was developed by a psychologist and psychotherapist called Eric Berne. His famous 'parent adult child' theory is still being developed today. TA has wide applications in clinical, therapeutic, organisational and personal development, covering communications, management, personality, relationships and behaviour. Whether you're in business, a parent, or interested in personal development, Eric Berne's theories, and those of his followers, will certainly bring new light to your dealings with people and your understanding of yourself.

So let's have a look at this theory and how it helps us frame questions that will allow us to become more assertive.

What are the roots of Transactional Analysis?

Throughout history, and from all perspectives - philosophy, medical science, religion - people have believed that each man and woman has a multiple nature.

In the early 20th century, Sigmund Freud first established that the human psyche is multi-faceted and that each of us has warring factions in our subconscious. We often say, for example, that part of me feels one way while part feels another way. Or, for example, that I wasn't feeling or acting myself this morning. Since then, new theories continue to be put forward, all concentrating on the essential principle that each one of us has parts of our personality which surface and affect our behaviour according to different circumstances.

In 1951 Dr Wilder Penfield began a series of scientific experiments. Using conscious human subjects, he proved that by touching a part of the brain (the temporal cortex) with a weak electrical probe, the brain could be triggered to 'play back' certain past experiences and the feelings associated with them. The patients 'replayed' these events and their feelings, despite not normally being able to recall them using their conventional memories.

Penfield's experiments continued over several years and resulted in wide acceptance of the following conclusions:

- The human brain acts like a tape recorder and while we may 'forget' experiences, the brain still has them recorded.

- Along with events the brain also records the associated feelings and both feelings and events remain locked together.

- It is possible for a person to exist in two states simultaneously (because patients replaying hidden events and feelings could talk about them objectively at the same time).

- Hidden experiences when replayed are vivid and affect how we feel at the time of replaying.

- There is a certain connection between mind and body, i.e. the link between the biological and the psychological, e.g. a psychological fear of spiders and a biological feeling of nausea.

In the 1950s Eric Berne began to develop his theories of Transactional Analysis. He said that verbal communication, particularly face to face, is at the centre of human social relationships and psychoanalysis.

His starting-point was that when two people encounter each other, one of them will speak to the other. This he called the Transaction Stimulus. The reaction from the other person he called the Transaction Response.

TA became the method of examining the transaction in which: 'I do something to you, and you do something back'.

Berne also said that each person is made up of three alter ego states:

- Parent
- Adult
- Child

These terms have different definitions from those used in everyday language.

Parent

The 'Parent' is our ingrained voice of authority, absorbed conditioning, learning and attitudes from when we were young. We were conditioned by our real parents, teachers, older people, next-door neighbours, aunts and uncles, Father Christmas and Jack Frost. Our Parent is made up of a huge number of hidden and overt recorded playbacks. Typically embodied by phrases and attitudes starting with 'how to', 'under no circumstances', 'always' and 'never forget', 'don't lie, cheat, steal' and so on. Our Parent is formed by external events and influences upon us as we grow through early childhood. We can change it, but this is easier said than done. When we are all being parental we all do this in different ways because we have had different experiences we are recalling

Child. Our internal reaction and feelings to external events form the 'Child'. This is the seeing, hearing, feeling, and emotional part within each of us. When anger or despair dominates reason, the Child is in control. Like our Parent we can change it, but it is no easier.

Adult. Our 'Adult' is our ability to think and determine action for ourselves, based on what we see going on. The Adult in us begins to form at around ten months old and is the means by which we keep our Parent and Child under control. If we are to change our Parent or Child we must do so through our adult.

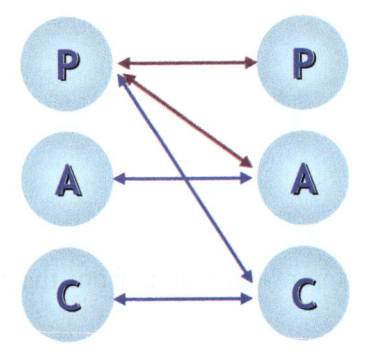

In other words:

- Parent is our 'Taught' perception of life.

- Adult is our 'Thought' perception of life.

- Child is our 'Felt' perception of life.

When we communicate, we are doing so from one of our own ego states: our Parent, Adult or Child. Our feelings at the time determine which one we use and at any time something can trigger a shift from one state to another. When we respond, we are also doing this from one of the three states and it is in the analysis of these stimuli and responses that the essence of Transactional Analysis lies.

At the core of Berne's theory is the rule that effective transactions (i.e. successful communications) must be complementary. They must go back from the receiving ego state to the sending ego state. For example, if the stimulus is Parent to Child, the response must be Child to Parent or the transaction is 'crossed' and there will be a problem between sender and receiver.

If a crossed transaction occurs, there is an ineffective communication. Worse still, either party or both will be upset. In order for the relationship to continue smoothly, the agent or the respondent must rescue the situation with a complementary transaction.

In serious breakdowns, there is no chance of immediately resuming a discussion about the original subject matter. Attention is focused on the relationship. The discussion can only continue constructively when and if the relationship is mended.

Here are some simple clues as to the ego state sending the signal. You will be able to see these clearly, both in others and in yourself:

Parent

- Physical - angry or impatient body-language and expressions, finger-pointing, patronising gestures,

- Verbal – 'Always', 'Never', 'For once and for all'; judgmental words, critical words, patronising language, posturing language.

N.B. beware of cultural differences in body-language or emphases that may appear 'Parental'.

Child

- Physical - emotionally sad expressions, despair, temper tantrums, whining voice, rolling eyes, shrugging shoulders, teasing, delight, laughter, speaking behind hand, raising hand to speak, squirming and giggling.

- Verbal - baby talk, 'I wish', 'I dunno', 'I want', 'I'm gonna', 'I don't care', 'Oh no, not again!', 'Things never go right for me', 'Worst day of my life!', 'Bigger', 'Biggest, 'Best'; many superlatives, words to impress.

Adult

- Physical - attentive, interested, straightforward, tilted head, non-threatening and non-threatened.

- Verbal – 'Why?', 'What?', 'How?', 'Who?', 'Where?' and 'When?', 'How much?', 'In what way?'; comparative expressions, reasoned statements, 'True', 'False', 'Probably', 'Possibly', 'I think', 'I realise', 'I see', 'I believe', 'In my opinion'.

And remember, when you are trying to identify ego states, words are only part of the story.

To analyse a transaction you need to see and feel what is being said as well.

- Only 7% of meaning is in the words spoken.
- 38% of meaning is paralinguistic (the way that the words are said).
- 55% is in facial expression.

(Source: Albert Mehrabian)

There is no general rule as to the effectiveness of any ego state in any given situation. Some people get results by being dictatorial (Parent to Child) or by having temper tantrums (Child to Parent). But for a balanced approach to life Adult to Adult is generally recommended.

TA can help you in every situation: firstly through being able to understand more clearly what is going on and secondly, by virtue of this knowledge, by giving ourselves choices of which ego states to adopt, which signals to send and where to send them. This enables us to make the most of all our communications and therefore to create, develop and maintain better relationships.

Transactional Analysis was developed significantly beyond Berne's early theories, by Berne himself until his death in 1970 and since then by his followers and many current experts in the field.

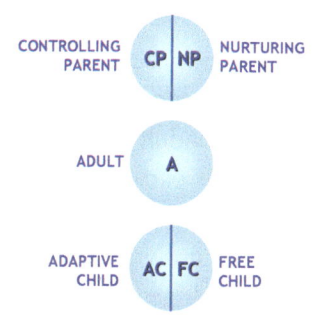

CONTROLLING PARENT CP | NP NURTURING PARENT

ADULT A

ADAPTIVE CHILD AC | FC FREE CHILD

Significantly, the original three Parent-Adult-Child components were sub-divided to form a new seven element model. This introduced Controlling and Nurturing aspects of the Parent mode, each with positive and negative aspects, and the Adapted and Free aspects of the Child mode, again each with positive and negative facets. This has provided us with the model to which most TA practitioners refer today:

Parent is now more commonly represented as a circle with two sections:

- **Nurturing** - Nurturing (positive) and Spoiling (negative).

- **Controlling** - Structuring (positive) and Critical (negative).

Adult remains as a single entity, representing a kind of 'mission control' mode, which can draw on the resources of both Parent and Child.

Child is now more commonly represented as a circle with two sections:

- **Adapted** - Co-operative when positive and compliant or resistant when negative.

- **Free** - Spontaneous when positive and immature when negative.

I'm sure that if you reflect on your recent behaviour you will easily be able to identify when you have been Parental or when you have been Childish or Child-like. Both the Adult and Child modes are ones we learned when we were in the early years of our development – typically before the age of eight. So when we are acting in this way we are replaying, maybe in a more grown up way (but not always), what we learned.

So, the assertive win-win relationship is Adult to Adult and that is what we should be aiming for most of the time. However we know that this is not always the game that is being played. When first exposed to this model, I quickly learned that if you are part of an 'unhealthy' game such as:

- A 'parental' boss talking down to you and not listening to your ideas or

- A childish team member not taking responsibility and consistently coming back to you with the same mistakes.

then *you* are part of the problem. These 'games' can only exist if you play your part in them. For your boss to be Parental to you then you must be in some way playing the Child and not being assertive.

Similarly if your team member is not taking responsibility, you are accepting this by being some kind of nurturing Parent.

While you may be part of the problem, this model provides us with clues as to how you can become part of the solution. You don't do this by arguing with the other person. You do it by asking questions that make:

- The Parent to realise he or she is being Parental.

- The Child to take responsibility be getting him or her to think through for themselves what they need to do and what choices they need to make.

So, let's look at a situation where you need to become more assertive and where someone else is playing (deliberately or not) the role of either a controlling or nurturing Parent. This could be, for example, when your boss is telling you the way she wants something done. She is very dogmatic about it and seemingly giving you little room to say what you want to say. You, on the other hand, are pretty sure that her proposal will not work in the way she is suggesting. How do you use questions in this scenario to allow you to modify the proposal?

Firstly, arguing directly is like trying to swim upstream against a strong current. If you want to cross the river you need to go with the current to some extent. So the questions you would need to ask would be ones that would come from your being in a more Adult problem-solving mode. You would need to ask questions that would help you understand why she feels so strongly and so inflexibly and by doing so make her realise that she might not be entirely right. This way, you show her you are interested and you also get more information. So great questions to ask might be:

- Can I just be clear on the outcome we are trying to achieve, so that I can make sure I go about this in the right way?

- Could you tell me specifically how your approach is going to work, as I'm not clear at the moment?

- I can see you feel strongly about this, what is making you so passionate about what you are suggesting?

Questions similar to this will help you both to understand what the objective is and the best way of achieving it without getting into an argument. For example, once you have mutual clarity concerning a task, and have thus established some rapport, it is likely to be much easier to get into a conversation about other ways of doing this. It is hard for your boss to stay in Parent mode when you are showing real interest and also asking questions to clarify the objective.

Of course, sometimes you have to deal with outright aggressive behaviour and the options seem to be either to stand and argue or to run away. I have found that one of the best ways to resolve this is to bring their behaviour to the attention of the aggressor and the effect this is having by asking a question. This question would look something like 'Can you tell me how your behaving this way is helping the situation?'

The best way of illustrating this is by an example. I was working with some senior nurses, helping them to become more assertive often in the face of consultants who were patronising to them. They, of course, spent a significant amount of time with the patients and had a lot to contribute while the consultants often had little more than 15-30 minutes a day. I realised that one of the nurses on the programme needed little help from me. She invited me to visit her ward for a few hours and, as it happened, I witnessed her in action dealing with a difficult consultant.

The consultant marched into the ward and came up to her and very loudly and aggressively, in front of patients and me, started criticising her for not freeing up some beds as he had ordered. She listened to this for a little while allowing him to hold forth. Then she quietly responded 'I know we need to free up beds and I am trying to do so, but can you tell me how speaking to me like this is going to help us achieve this?' The effect was immediate. He apologised and suggested they go into her office and discuss things properly

Looking at a situation the other way round and considering how to persuade someone who is not taking responsibility to become more assertive is the subject of the following chapter.

What Might You Have Learned In This Chapter About Using Questions To Become More Assertive?

- In what situations would it be useful to become more assertive?
- Where and when do you find yourself in the 'Child' ego state?
- What is the value of asking questions here rather than arguing your point?

Top 10 Questions To Help You To Promote Assertiveness

1. What makes you feel so strongly about this?
2. Could you tell me specifically how your proposal might work?
3. What are we trying to achieve here?
4. How is your proposal helping to achieve this outcome?
5. What other ways have you considered?
6. What might be the impact of this on…..?
7. How is behaving in this way helping here?
8. What do you need to resolve this?
9. How can we work more effectively in the future?
10. How can I take more responsibility here?

How Can Questions Grow Responsibility?

In the last chapter we looked at how you can become more assertive. The converse of this is, of course, how can you help *others* to become more assertive and to take responsibility. This is when, going back to the Parent-Adult-Child model in the previous chapter, they have been used to acting in the Child mode.

An automatic response here, if we 'play the game', is for us to become either the nurturing Parent, accepting their shortcomings and supporting them, or to become the controlling Parent, trying autocratically to order them to do something. Neither strategy will be successful in building responsibility. You are still the person doing all the work, doing most of the speaking and in the end having to monitor or make adjustments for their lack of performance

What we need to do is to get them to work things out and make the choices for themselves. You can't *tell* people to become responsible. But you can help them become more responsible by making them think through their actions by asking great questions.

In this chapter we look at a model called the GROW model. While no one person can be clearly identified as the originator Graham Alexander, Alan Fine, Sir John Whitmore, who are well known in the world of coaching, made significant contributions.

It's a model that shows you when to ask the right questions in order to take someone from simply having a problem through to taking action. It has stood the test of time as it has been around a number of years.

The GROW Model

The GROW model, shown here diagrammatically, is a simple but powerful process for building responsibility in others. A good way of thinking about the GROW Model is to consider how you'd plan a journey. First, you decide where you are going (the goal) and establish where you currently are (your current reality).

You then explore various routes (the options) to your destination. In the final step, establishing the will, you ensure that you're committed to making the journey and are prepared for the obstacles that you could meet on the way.

The GROW model can be a formal process that takes a lot of dedicated time. But, often, it need only take just a few minutes asking a few open questions. You will be amazed at the results, especially the increased responsibility and motivation of those at the receiving end.

This process is perfect for someone who has some knowledge of how to accomplish the task but needs help getting to the stage when they can take full responsibility. As a leader, your job is to make sure that clarity regarding what and why - and especially competence in how - are in place.

_G_OALS   First, you and the other person need to look at the behaviour that you want to change and then to structure this change as a goal that they want to achieve. When doing this, it's useful to ask questions like 'How will you know that your team member has achieved this goal?' and 'How will you know that the problem or issue is solved?'

REALITY Next, help the other person to describe their current reality. This is an important step. Too often, people try to solve a problem or reach a goal without fully considering their starting point and often they're missing some information that they need in order to reach their goal effectively. As they tell you about their current reality, the solution may start to emerge.

OPTIONS Once you have explored the current reality, it's time to determine what is possible - meaning all of the possible options for reaching her objective. Help them brainstorm as many good options as possible. Then, discuss these and help them to decide on the best ones. By all means, offer your own suggestions in this step. But let the other person offer suggestions first and let them do most of the talking. It's important to guide them in the right direction, without actually making decisions for them.

WRAP UP By examining the current reality and exploring the options, the other person will now have a good idea of how they can achieve their goal. That's great - but in itself, this may not be enough. The final step is to get them to commit to specific actions in order to move forward towards their goal. In doing this, you will help them establish their commitment and boost their motivation.

GOALS

When possible it is useful to plan any discussion using this process. With skill and practice it will become more and more of an automatic process.

The following is a list of points to consider at this stage of the process:

- As a leader or manager you may have a long term and/or short term goal or outcome for the process.

- It is likely to be useful to consider the development level of the other person and therefore your leadership style, though it will be important to be prepared to be flexible. As their development level increases they will need to have more ownership of the goal.

- Think of this stage as getting to 'Yes! Yes! Yes!' If necessary, start at big picture level where you are likely to reach agreement (e.g. company goals or performance needs). Then gradually chunk down, getting agreement as you go. Achieving this is the foundation for the rest of the process. Without solid foundations the rest could crumble!

- Ensure at the end of this stage that you have agreed an outcome and that it is positive. Summarise to ensure you both agree.

TIP: although you might start to get into the next stage of the GROW process as part of agreeing goals, control this as much as possible. Recognise any points raised and write them down, but suggest that first of all you need to agree what you are trying to achieve.

REALITY

This stage is about agreeing where the other person is now. At the end of this stage you will both have agreed where you are going - the outcome or goal - and where you are now. With these in place you will find that the subsequent stages become much easier. The following are a list of points to consider:

- Ask what the other person thinks the situation is. This is a good way to check the development level. If they do not seem to be very clear then their development level is likely to be lower and they need more direction than coaching.

- Check any assumptions you have made. For example, say 'I noticed ... and I wondered if this aspect might be causing a problem'.

- Summarise at the end of this stage to check for agreement.

OPTIONS

This stage is likely to prove the most positive and relaxed especially when the first two stages have been well managed and agreed. You might want to consider the following points: -

- The development level of the other person will have a big influence on their level of contribution.

- It is sometimes useful, especially in more difficult situations, to write all ideas down. Use brainstorming rules where appropriate.

- End this stage having agreed what options you have both chosen

- This is where you can add some of your own ideas - as long as you ensure the other person really does make the choice of options.

WRAP UP

Even if you are on the right track, you will get run over if you just sit there.

Will Rogers

During this stage you ensure that any actions are agreed and that a time to review progress is set. Unless you review progress much of the good work you have accomplished may go to waste. Remember not to 'feed your monkey' by taking on responsibility for actions you could easily delegate. You don't build responsibility by taking it away. When developing actions consider:

1. What they can do?

2. What it is essential that you do?

3. What they might want others to do?

Examples of Useful Questions when Using 'Grow'

Goal

- What is it you would like to discuss?

- What would you like to achieve?

- What would you like from (to achieve in) this session?

- What would need to happen for you to walk away feeling that this time was well spent?

- If I could grant you a wish for this session, what would it be?

- What would you like to be different when you leave this session?

- What would you like to happen that is not happening now or what would you like not to happen that is happening now?

- What outcome would you like from this session/discussion/interaction? Is that realistic?

- Can we do that in the time we have available?

- Will that be of real value to you?

Reality

- What is happening at this moment?

- How do you know that this is accurate?

- When does this happen?

- How often does this happen? Be as precise if possible.

- What effect does this have?

- How have you verified, or would you verify, that that is so?

- What other factors are relevant?

- Who else is relevant?

- What is their perception of the situation?

- What have you tried so far?

How Can Questions Grow Responsibility?

- What would you rather have?
- How will you know if you have got it?
- Is it in your control?
- If you could have your outcome would you take it?

Options

- What could you do to change the situation?
- What alternatives are there to that approach?
- Tell me what possibilities for action you see. Don't worry whether they are realistic now.
- What approach/actions have you seen used, or used yourself, in similar circumstance?
- Who might be able to help?
- Would you like suggestions from me?
- Which options do you like the most?
- What are the benefits and pitfalls of these options?
- Which options are of interest to you?
- Rate from 1-10 your interest level in/the practicality of each of these options.
- Would you like to choose an option to act on?

Wrap-up

- What are the next steps?
- Precisely when will you taken them?
- What might get in the way?
- Do you need to log the steps in your diary?
- What support do you need?
- How and when will you enlist that support

Building responsibility and awareness in others is one of the most important things that you can do as a manager. It requires an investment in time, but the time you gain by not having to do the job yourself and the satisfaction delivered on both sides when someone develops more of their potential, is well worth it

When you start using this model, or even parts of it, keep it simple. In fact, at the end of this book there is a list of questions called the Million Dollar Questions. These are very much based on the GROW model and I have found that simply by having these in front of you, and asking each in turn, you will experience significant success. Remember it is highly unlikely you can do any harm by asking questions and listening to the other person!

It is also easy to develop your own list of question taken from the examples I have listed.

How Can Questions Grow Responsibility?

What Might You Have Learned In This Chapter About Using Questions To Develop Responsibility In Others?

- How important is it to develop responsibility?
- What is the main 'plank' of developing responsibility in others?
- How can you use the GROW model to help build responsibility?

Top 10 Questions To Help You To Promote Responsibility

1. What makes you feel so strongly about this?
2. Could you tell me specifically how your proposal might work?
3. What are we trying to achieve here?
4. How is your proposal helping to achieve this outcome?
5. What other ways have you considered?
6. What might be the impact of this on ...?
7. How is behaving in this way helping here?
8. What do you need to resolve this?
9. How can we work more effectively in the future?
10. How can I take more responsibility here?

What Could I Learn About Listening?

> No one ever listened themselves out of a job.
>
> **Calvin Coolidge**

So, we've all learned about the importance of asking great questions. But, what about listening skills? Why do so many people crave the company of a good listener?

My Dad died in late 2012. He had been very much involved in community activities all his life - as a councillor, chairman of charities, etc. and involvement in protest groups. At his funeral many people came up to me and said nice things about him. But the common theme was not what he had achieved, but that he always had time for people. What a legacy!

In the first few years of life, we all learn to speak. In fact, it's a significant developmental milestone, a sign that a child is developing normally. However, listening is an equally important skill that is often overlooked by parents and educators - and bosses.

Yes, we were all taught (hopefully) to listen to our parents and to listen in school. However, few of us were taught *effective* listening skills - the active, disciplined kind of listening that helps us examine and challenge the information we hear, thereby improving our decision-making.

I know that when I'm coaching someone the only time I'm stuck for a question to ask is when I haven't been listening properly in the first place and I've let my mind wander. If I have been listening carefully, the next question is usually obvious.

What Can I Learn About Listening?

Most people want to be heard, but paradoxically very few people are good at listening. Learning to listen offers benefits both on and off the job.

Often when running a session on leadership I ask the group to list the names of three people they regard as being really good listeners. I then ask them if anyone has written the name of a person they don't like. It is very rare for anyone to answer yes here unless it's out of envy.

Then I ask if the three people whose names they have written would be included in any one of these categories:

- Liked by them

- Loved by them

- Respected by them

Again, nearly everyone can put the names into any one of these categories and sometimes all three! The message from this is clear: people who listen well not only benefit from really hearing what the other person says but enjoy the double whammy of being liked, respected or even loved for it.

One of Stephen Covey's 'Seven Habits of Highly Effective People' is to listen first to understand, before trying to be understood. This works on the two levels discussed. Firstly, it builds respect and empathy with the talker and, secondly, it gives you information and often (very importantly) time to understand what is really going on and to frame your questions accordingly.

Recent work on neuroscience has also demonstrated the power and benefit of really listening. In David Rock's book 'Your Brain at Work' he shows in his SCARF model that status is a key need for all of us. If we think our status is not recognised (and I'm not talking about money or position, but existence as a person with a right to have a view) then this triggers the basic emotional response of fight or flight

Simply put, most people are terrible at listening. People tend to spend more time evaluating what the speaker is saying or mentally composing their responses than they do actually listening. The fact that so few people are good listeners means that people who do possess this rare skill set have several advantages. Here are six:

Respect When you listen with full attention, you are communicating respect. By offering speakers respect, you gain theirs.

Airtime If you listen first, others are more likely to return the favour. There will always be people who, because of stress, self-absorption or other reasons, will bend another person's ear and not return the favour. Nevertheless, the great majority of individuals understand there should be give and take in conversation.

Information Attentive listening helps you learn more about other people. Knowing more about people is helpful in your professional life as well as personal life. Imagine the benefits when you understand your boss, colleagues, customers, spouse, friends, and family members better.

Increased Likability Even people who aren't shameless narcissists crave attention. People like people who listen. You may also find that as you listen to people more, you like them more.

Better Relationships Listening creates a feeling of goodwill in intimate and professional relationships.

Improve your relationships by listening non-judgmentally to the concerns and problems of others. The more you listen without judgment, the more freedom speakers have to find their own solutions to problems.

Greater Clarity Careful listening helps you avoid some of the confusion, misunderstandings and conflicts that commonly arise in conversations. Careful listening offers an opportunity to circumvent the usual arguments and conversation traps.

The benefits of listening are mutually supportive – the more you acquire the benefits of good listening, the more listening you will do and the more the other benefits will start to pile up. As with most other social skills, to master listening, you need to practice. The world is full of people who feel unheard and believe no one is paying attention to them, so you have plenty of opportunities.

In my early days as a manager I had a member of staff who would talk incessantly. It seemed to me to be such a waste of time to discuss at such length issues the solutions to which were patently obvious. I became increasingly frustrated in how to deal with her. Then a wise colleague said to me, after listening to me complaining about her, 'Perhaps she needs a good listening to'. I realised that maybe the reason she was talking so much was that she didn't feel she was being listened to. So I did just that and spent an hour with her just really listening, showing attention and curiosity. Guess what! It didn't resolve things completely, but the situation improved significantly.

However, there are different types of listening. The first type I will refer to as Level One. This is where, even though you are listening to what the other person is saying, you are processing that information in order to recall similar experiences and then, when you get the opportunity, you jump in and relate them. This may be OK for conversations in a pub with friends and is more about entertainment than constructive learning. My father in law used to call them 'top 'em' conversations. One person would relate an experience and the other would tell people about his or her better, bigger, more dangerous experience!

An amusing example is this excerpt from a famous Monty Python sketch:

1st YORKSHIREMAN: Aye, very passable, that, very passable bit of risotto.

2nd YORKSHIREMAN: Nothing like a good glass of Château de Chasselas, eh, Josiah?

3rd YORKSHIREMAN: You're right there, Obadiah.

4th YORKSHIREMAN: Who'd have thought thirty year ago we'd all be sittin' here drinking Château de Chasselas, eh?

1st YORKSHIREMAN: In them days we was glad to have the price of a cup o' tea.

2nd YORKSHIREMAN: A cup o' cold tea.

4th YORKSHIREMAN: Without milk or sugar.

3rd YORKSHIREMAN: Or tea.

1st YORKSHIREMAN: In a cracked cup, an' all.

4th YORKSHIREMAN: Oh, we never had a cup. We used to have to drink out of a rolled up newspaper.

2nd YORKSHIREMAN: The best we could manage was to suck on a piece of damp cloth.

What Can I Learn About Listening?

> 3rd YORKSHIREMAN: But you know, we were happy in those days, though we were poor.

An exercise I often use in development programmes demonstrates both the power of listening well and how people feel when they are not being listened to. I split the group into pairs and I ask one person to be the speaker talking about something they are interested in or passionate about. I take the 'listeners' outside the room and brief them. I tell them for the first couple of minutes to pay attention and act as though they were really interested. I then give them a sign after which they gradually, and then more obviously, become distracted by looking away, writing on a piece of paper, checking their phones and so on.

I let the exercise run for a bit and then stop it before fighting broke out! The feedback from the speakers was that initially they really enjoyed being listened to and found it easy to talk. But when attention was taken away they became annoyed, even angry and their talking just dried up.

I am not saying there is necessarily anything wrong with level one listening. It may be great for friends at the pub chatting about nothing of any real importance. But when it comes to real discussion and real understanding a different level of listening is needed.

This we will call Level Two. At this level we are listening with curiosity to what the other person is saying. We are trying to understand where they are coming from. It is at this level where most of the benefits lie. If we are trying to influence the other person with questions we need to fully understand, not just the words someone is saying, but how they are saying them and the energy behind what is being said. This requires skill and concentration.

The following simple components, familiar to all of us while we are at our best, are all part of a single activity: drawing out the speaker's real views and opinions:

- Paying attention
- Reflecting
- Incorporating feeling
- Checking
- Clarifying and verifying conclusions
- Summarising
- Asking for examples
- Encouraging
- Showing Empathy
- Questioning
- Silence

Paying Attention

It is surprising how ineffectual we are at showing others that we are paying attention to what they are saying. Experience shows that people unintentionally show more detachment than they realise. We become preoccupied with taking notes and thinking about what we want to say or ask next. And in formal interviews and meetings we often use a non-committal tone of voice with too little eye contact. It is important that we demonstrate to others that we are listening. An important part of this is body posture:

- More leaning forward than back
- More face-on to the speaker than sideways
- Good eye contact
- Generally relaxed

... and, finally

- Listening to the end of the sentence.

This last is important. Too often we assume we know how the speaker will complete his sentence and are already thinking about how we will formulate our response. It is at the end of sentences that we often find the caveats to what has been said, such as...

'...maybe.' or *'...I don't know.'* or *'...it's all just the flavour of the month anyway.'*

These little caveats are often the indicators of where the hidden agenda lies and what it might be. We need to pay attention right to the end of the sentence to catch these nuances.

Reflecting

It is important to reflect back to the speaker what he has said:

'So, you're committed to the work but you don't think you have enough time to prepare effectively?'

A reflection should be a simple paraphrase of what the speaker has said. The purpose is to make the point succinctly in a way that prompts him to say

'Yes, and....' or *'Yes, because ...'.*

Phrases to avoid here are:

'Yes, but...'

'If I understood you correctly...'

'So what you are really saying is...'

'I hear what you are saying'

Incorporating feeling

Speakers' feelings are often not expressed directly but are plainly there. It is often useful to bring them out into the open. Acknowledging them often opens up the speaker to talk about what really is on his mind:

'So you've taken on a high profile project that you have to deliver in a very short timescale and your director has high expectations. You must feel exposed?'

The speaker will often reply:

'Yes, that's exactly how I feel. You see .....'

It is important to avoid incorporating feelings here that are already acknowledged by the speaker.

Checking

The last two examples illustrated the process of checking that you heard or understood the speaker correctly. But you can do it more explicitly:

'Did you say your director has high expectations of your project?'

Clarifying and verifying conclusions

In the context of a formal interview people sometimes feel it is inappropriate to admit they do not understand something. However it is valuable to say, when necessary:

'I did not quite understand that. Were you implying that your director is deliberately putting pressure on you?'

This is valuable because not only does it ensure you have picked up the right messages but also it demonstrates that you want to understand.

Summarising

This is a key technique. It allows you to keep track of what the speaker is saying:

'So, let's see if I've got this right. You have this high profile project. The director is putting pressure on you and you're trying to do your annual budget. You feel exposed as you don't feel you will be able to do justice to the project. Is that right?'

It also serves to slow the speaker down and reflect a little on what he or she has said. This slowing down can be quite important for those individuals who have a lot on their mind. Summarising can often present them with a number of threads, which they may choose to follow:

'Yes that's right. I hate budgeting; it's not my strong point'

This quite often is an effective route to identifying what might really be bothering the speaker. Note, though, that if the speaker is experiencing a lot of anger and frustration, it is best to allow him to give vent to that, even if it means you have to keep quiet for ten minutes or so. Only when the speaker has run out of steam is it sensible to work back through what has been said to see if you have understood correctly.

> *A wise old owl lived in an oak,*
> *The more he saw the less he spoke*
> *The less he spoke the more he heard.*
> *Why can't we all be like that wise old bird?*

Asking for examples

It is always useful to get a concrete example that illustrates what the individual is talking about:

'You implied you were not very good at budgeting. Can you give an example of how you are bad at budgeting?'

or

'You said the director was putting pressure on you. Can you give me an example of how he is doing that?'

> *Conversation is an exchange of knowledge. Argument is an exchange of ignorance.*
>
> **Author Unknown**

> *As friends, we don't see eye to eye, but then we don't hear ear to ear either.*
>
> **Buster Keaton**

Encouragers

Sometimes called lubricators, these are essentially gestures that encourage the individual in what he is saying. Encouragers can be non-verbal:

- Nodding

- Looking suddenly more intent

- Raising an eyebrow.

Encouragers can also be utterances such as:

- 'Uh huh'

- 'Mmm...mm'

- 'I see'

Showing Empathy

Empathy is a common human quality. Recent research from neuroscience shows we have these things called mirror neurons that make us want to copy and mirror others' behaviours and feelings. Empathy is not the same as sympathy. Sympathy is about sharing the feeling with someone.

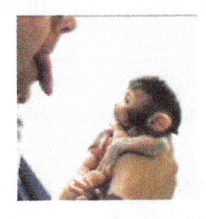

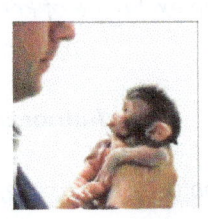

Empathy is simply recognising another's feelings often by simply saying 'I Understand'.

Questions

Questions are a more elaborate and directed form of encouragement. Questions should be aimed at bringing out the speaker. The objective is to open out the boundaries of what the speaker is saying.

You need to avoid closed questions here. You also need to avoid too much probing on a single issue at this stage as it might close out other avenues that need to be explored. Get the complete picture before you begin focusing on particular areas.

Silence

Silence can feel uncomfortable and we are often tempted to fill it. The gap above illustrates the point. We sometimes fill silences even before they occur. We may persistently rephrase our question because we fear that the other person will not respond and there will be a silence. This leads to multiple questions, which at best serve to give the other person a choice of questions to answer or at worst confuse and irritate them.

Sir Lawrence Olivier was once asked what was the secret of his acting success. He went quiet for what seemed an uncomfortably long time before replying (with a slight smile, I imagine) 'I'm good at pauses'.

Do not be afraid of silence. Silences are usually shorter than they seem and often put more pressure on the speaker than the listener.

Please read the following questions and then select the answers that fit best.. (I'm sure your answers will be honest ones … you wouldn't wish to fool yourself!) I have found by just looking at the questions it helps identify good and bad habits.

	Almost always	Often	Sometimes	Not often	Almost Never
1. I give my full attention to the person who is talking to me.					

What Can I Learn About Listening?

2.	When listening to a speaker, I make eye contact.				
3.	If what the speaker is saying doesn't interest me, my mind wanders.				
4.	I nod my head in agreement with what a speaker is saying.				
5.	I tend to daydream or let my mind wander when listening to others.				
6.	If I'm unsure of whether I've grasped a point correctly, I summarize my understanding back to the speaker to confirm that I've got it right.				
7.	I find myself thinking about what I'm going to say next, while a speaker is talking to me.				
8.	I fidget or drum my fingers on a surface when I listen to others speaking.				
9.	I can block out background noise when a speaker is talking.				
10.	I bite my nails or pen while I listen to someone speaking with me.				
11.	If I'm bored or uninterested in what someone is saying to me, I look at the ground or my feet.				
12.	If someone says something I don't approve of, I make disapproving faces.				

13. I wait for a speaker to finish their point before making a mental judgement on what they said.				
14. I immediately correct a speaker if they mispronounce a word.				
15. I try to divert or end conversations that don't interest me.				
16. I get bored if I'm not the one leading a conversation, for example, choosing the topic or controlling the pace.				
17. I ask questions to encourage a speaker to elaborate a point.				
18. If someone doesn't get straight to the point, I become impatient e.g. I tap my feet, look around or check my watch.				
19. People complain that I don't look like I'm listening when they talk to me.				
20. I briefly pause and think over what a speaker has said before replying.				
21. I summarize out loud what a speaker has said after they finish talking.				
22. I find it difficult to focus on the message if a speaker uses poor grammar.				
23. I use confirmation noises e.g. 'I see', 'uh huh', 'go on' etc. to encourage someone to continue speaking.				

What Can I Learn About Listening?

24. If I disagree with something someone is saying I will stop the speaker mid-sentence to give my opinion.				
25. If I have something relevant to add to the conversation, I find it difficult to wait until the other person has finished speaking.				
26. If a speaker is venting their emotions, I wait until they have let it all out before commenting.				
27. I play close attention to the speaker's body language.				
28. If a speaker says something I really disagree with, I make a disapproving sound e.g. a groan or 'tsk'.				
29. I face the speaker fully when listening and will stop other tasks to look at them.				
30. If there are others talking around me, I can't help but listen in on their conversations as well as the one I'm taking part in.				
31. I finish other people's sentences for them.				
32. I would interrupt a serious discussion to take a personal call.				

33. I ask a speaker to repeat themselves because I can't remember a point they made earlier in the conversation.				
34. I tune out momentarily and have to ask a speaker to repeat a point that I missed.				
35. When a speaker is talking to me on the telephone I think about something completely un-related to the conversation I am having.				
36. I work on the computer while someone is talking to me on the telephone.				

Real Examples From Leaders

In this chapter I have included the many example of questions that have been sent to me by friends and colleagues. I have attributed them to the people that sent me them. Each one hopefully has some context and comment on what happened as a result. I have also commented on why I think that question worked

The purpose of this is to show how many different examples there are and how easy it is to develop the ones that can work for you with a little thought.

On my website you will see many other examples and please feel to add your own. I may include them in future editions

Lord Butler of Brocknell, Master of University College Oxford, former Secretary of the Cabinet and Head of the Home Civil Service.

How would you like me to change the way I do my job?

Comment – Puts the onus on the receiver to be very specific about change rather than imply general dissatisfaction

Frances Heaton, Non-Executive Director Commercial Union, Legal & General, formerly of the Court of the Bank of England and Director General of the Takeover Panel

How would you change the way it has always been done? What are the alternatives?

Comment – Puts the responsibility on the receiver to come up with a positive response rather than complain

David Salisbury – CEO dimensional Fund Advisors ltd

What are our prospective clients trying to achieve when they purchase our services? And similarly what are they hoping to achieve when they purchase our competitors' services? What is our value-added? In which areas of the market do these two coincide?

Comment – The first step in leadership is being prepared to admit that you don't have the answers. Ironically you find your way by admitting you don't know the way

Sir Julian Oswald, Chairman Aerosytems, Green Issues, Past Chairman of SEMA Group plc. Director Marine and General Mutual Life Insurance.

What is stopping me/you doing better?

Comment – this question frames the issue of whether or not I or anyone else can do better, assumes we can (which will always be right) and set us thinking - How?

Steve Toft – PricewaterhouseCoopers

What conversation am I avoiding today?

I know that avoiding difficult decisions is one of my worst management faults. I can find all sorts of reasons to avoid those decisions that I would then have to execute. I am, by the way, excellent at spotting, and pointing out to them, the difficult decisions that others need to make and execute! My problem, I argue to myself, lies in not wanting to hurt. What I have eventually understood however is that by avoiding the immediate hurt, I simply create it in spades further down the line, and indeed it is often spread more widely than would have happened if I had tackled that difficult decision as it arose.

So over the years I have got much braver and tougher on myself, and most times when I know I am in avoidance I take a deep breath and go for it. (Note that I do this most times, but by no means all!).

Comment - This is an action-based question. If we could ask ourselves, our team, or those that report to us, this question each morning, and get an honest answer, many management decisions would be made earlier and in the overall interest of the business and its people.

Being honest about this question is hard. Bluntly, however, we design poor plans, wrongly invest money, hire and fire people without good cause, waste energy, and do many other inappropriate things, often just because we are too scared to face a truth and would rather construct another reality to live by.

Christine Watson - Founder of Blu-Sky Coaching and ex HR Director of Hewlett Packard

What are the benefits of not achieving this?

Comment – there are hidden benefits in every situation, especially in staying as you are; you just need to look for them. Once these benefits are identified you can often find other ways to satisfy them and achieve the goal you want more easily. If you are not aware of them it can be a struggle to change anything

Lorraine Steele - Director Steele Consulting

'What is the longest you have gone without drinking coffee?'

I drink too much coffee and having a kidney problem so really I 'should' not drink coffee. I get tired of doctors, specialist, homeopaths and friend wagging their advice giving finger at me and say 'why do you drink it. You really should stop'

Well - I was at a new homeopath and she started asking me about my coffee intake and I thought, 'oh here goes, the lecture about coffee,' and instead she asked: *'What is the longest you have gone without drinking coffee?'*

Well, It completely turned it around for me. I was so intrigued and so relived to not get the 'naughty child' lecture that I woke up the next morning and did not drink it all day long. I wanted to see what was the longest - I went for 6 days - then went to Italy with my husband (hard to avoid coffee in Italy). Now I only drink it on weekends or every other day. So my behaviour has permanently changed based on one question.

Comment: A brilliant example of the difference asking a good question makes compared to giving advice. I intend to ask myself this except about eating chocolate

Wanda Bridge, Group Head of HR and Recruitment, Medex Scientific (UK) Ltd

So what?

This was prompted in a coaching session when the person was describing a messy situation with lots of 'they did that', 'he said this', 'she thought that', etc., etc. The person was upset and agitated about the situation and how others were reacting, and what they were thinking. 'So what?' was asked in a soft calm tone. It stopped them in their tracks, made them think if any of it really mattered or not and enabled them to pull out what was important and what wasn't with the situation and how to move forward from there.

Comment: Sometimes questions can be very short as in this example where it almost doesn't seem to be a question. I'm sure this question emerged because Wanda was also listening very carefully

David Clutterbuck - Author & Visiting professor to the coaching and mentoring faculties of both Oxford Brookes University and Sheffield Hallam University

So help me understand your motivations here?

Always maintain respect for the other person and help them maintain their own self-respect. Phrase challenging questions in ways that don't undermine their self-esteem. 'So help me understand your motivations here?' Rather than: 'Don't you think that's being a bit selfish? If people feel criticised they are likely to become defensive.

Comment: Also great way of also suspending any assumptions you may have about what's going on.

Elizabeth Cardy – Executive Coach

'Who are you trying to please?'

I use this question occasionally with clients who work all the time and want to get their lives back in balance; or with perfectionists, or those who never put themselves first.

I used it once with a senior scientist who was seeking a promoted post in his organisation; this was a man who was highly analytical, questioned everything (including my questions to him and, I discovered, his interviewers at interview). He paid no attention to feelings, seeing no relevance to his quest for promotion. This question suddenly got his (deceased) parents and god into the room, and the coaching took a different turn. It lead to discussion about his core drivers, impact on others, and self-presentation. He went on to succeed at a subsequent interview and is still operating at a senior level.

Comment: What a great example of a very open and concise question. It also shows that you never know what will arise when you ask something like that and in this case it was obviously a breakthrough

Tomas Peters - COO at ING Commercial Banking

Did your day matter?

I always liked the question my former boss asked me when he saw me at the end of the day. He asked 'Did your day matter?'

I liked that, given that on many days executives are only attending meetings and representing, but if you focus on what really matters, time management gets easier and your team and peers will notice that you focus on what really matters.

Comment: An example of a simple question that gets you to focus. Having read it I also can't stop asking myself that question. Thank you Tomas

Martijn Rademakers - MD - Centre For Strategy & Leadership, Rotterdam

How about the opposite?

I have an extremely simple question to share: 'How about the opposite?'

The question helps my discussion partners and I avoid tunnel vision in discussions about solutions to complex issues.

Comment: It's easy to think you have made a great decision when you have nothing to compare it with. When confronted with an option you then have to think through why your original idea was the best

Lillian Ballering – CEO Movimento raad & daad bv

Imagine the program is delivered successfully: What will have been the main issues that you have overcome?

I use this question when getting a project team to think through the risks of the project

Comment: Getting people into the mindset of looking back from success rather than looking forward often helps people discuss things in a more relaxed and open way

John Bull CEO Tall Tree

'How good are these guys - Really, how good are they?'

It's not just a rugby game it's Australia v All Blacks in Sydney 1994. Australia are fielding an awesome side, which the All Blacks (a young side) fear. In the 1st half, Australia dominates all areas of the game, score 3 tries and lead 20: 0

At the half time chat Laurie Mains the All Blacks coach starts his team talk asking: 'How good are these guys - Really, how good are they?'...and then he walked out!

In the second half the All Blacks look like they have fielded a new team - but it's the same 15 men. They score 2 sensational tries, converting both and a penalty to come within striking range with 15 minutes left. The Aussies are just stunned! The third try for the All Blacks – or not, as it happens as when certain to score the clincher they are thwarted by a magnificent tackle and the Aussies win 20:16

Comment: Great example of how a simple question can get a team of people to re-examine their assumptions and behave differently

Alex Ferguson - Previous Manager Manchester United

'What do you think they're talking about in their changing room?'

United were 2:0 up at half time against their arch-rivals, Liverpool, and strolling. At half time Fergie walked into the dressing room and asked his team, who were all relaxed and talking about how easy it was:

'What do you think they're talking about in their changing room?'

As you can imagine this changed the mood and got them talking on how they would deal with Liverpool's expected response. United won 2:0

Comment: For once not the hair dryer treatment but equally as effective

Chris Billingham- Programme Manager - Kohler Mira Ltd.

What would you do in my position?

Recently our (live in) au pair of 2 years accepted a job as we were coming to the end of the contract. She didn't even discuss the implications that she was finishing 2 weeks early, leaving our children and us in a difficult position! It certainly made her stop and think about the impact on others where she had been totally focused on her own point of view.

Comment: A great way of getting someone to think differently without getting into an argument

Peter Bregman - Coach and Contributor to HBR

What can I do, right now that would be the most powerful use of this moment?

It's not that we're lazy. We put effort into what we do. I ran on the treadmill every day. But, like my daily run, our efforts often don't translate into optimum results.

The basic principle is simple: We're already spending a certain amount of time doing things - in meetings, managing businesses, writing emails, making decisions. If we could just make a higher impact during that time, it's all upside with no cost. So here's the question I'd like to propose you ask yourself throughout your day:

What can I do, right now that would be the most powerful use of this moment?

What can I say? What action can I take? What question can I ask? What issue can I bring up? What decision can I make that would have the greatest impact?

Comment: Such a great question – I use it as often as I have the courage to

How Can I Start?

Many people I meet say that it is one thing knowing how powerful a skilled questions can be, but it is entirely another being able to do this at the right time to the people you want to. What stops them?

It may be any number of reasons but most often quoted are:

- In a group or meeting often a few individuals will dominate proceedings and it is very difficult to get a word in

- The meeting may be going down a particular avenue that you believe is wrong and it feels hard to pull them up abruptly with a question that might alter their direction significantly. Even if you do you feel your intervention is likely to be ignored because it is against the momentum of the moment

- Others never seem to really listen to the points you make or take little notice

- The person you are addressing you perceive for many reasons to be far more powerful and experienced than you. Who are you to challenge such a person?

There is no simple solution to these problems but there are some strategies and ways of thinking that from our experience and our observation of others have proved useful. You might find them of use too.

Firstly lets deal with the 'I am not worthy' issue. From my introduction to the history of questions it is clear that there is no such thing as absolute knowledge. You have a perfect right to ask someone a question to check out their assumptions. If they are not prepared to be challenged it is likely that this says more about them than you.

How Can I Start?

Rather than viewing those who ask questions as lacking knowledge, people who ask powerful questions tend to be seen as leaders in learning and making things happen.

I am often inspired in these situations by the words of Marianne Williamson quoted by that wonderful statesman Nelson Mandela in his inaugural speech:

'Our deepest fear is not that we are inadequate. Our deepest fear is that we are powerful beyond measure. It is our light not our darkness that most frightens us.'

'We ask ourselves who am I to be brilliant, gorgeous, talented and fabulous. Actually who are you not to be? You are a child of god your playing small does not serve the world. There is nothing enlightened about shrinking so that other people won't feel insecure around you.'

'We are born to manifest the glory of god that is within us. Its not just in some of us its in everyone, and as we let our own light shine we unconsciously give other people permission to do the same. As we are liberated from our own fear our presence automatically liberates others.'

It is likely of course that they might find it difficult to admit they don't know all the answers. It is important to recognise that this might be an issue and asking a skilful question can allow the other person space to retreat from their position without having to admit weakness.

For example asking why someone thinks the way they do is very direct and quite threatening as we showed in the last section. However asking a question more like 'Can you tell me what has led you to that conclusion?'

Asking the right questions also means you are prepared to listen to the answers. If your intent in asking a question is to belittle someone or show them how clever you are you are unlikely to be making the improvement you need. It is difficult to hide your intent from others and if you are not honest in yours they will respond accordingly.

If you want to be better at asking more and better questions there is no alternative but to practice. Matthew Syed in his book 'Bounce' proposes that there is no such thing as talent. He demonstrates that anyone in any walk of life is good at what they do because they practice and practice.

So how will you start practising? As we talked about in the chapter on getting into action momentum is a wonderful thing and starting small and keeping going is key.

Lastly I often wonder why it is that when someone is promoted, they start to change their behaviour. All the interpersonal skills they had to use to achieve things when they had little power seem to go out of the window.

Below are some of the factors that help explain this. In becoming aware of these factors, both as leaders and as those that help develop leaders in our organisations, we can strive to avoid pitfalls and help focus on the behaviours that have been proved time and again to be far more effective in delivering sustained benefits in this complex world. And I hope you will have realised asking questions is a powerful way out of this dilemma

1. Those in a power role are often removed from the checks and balances of the feedback loop in which people tell each other about their impact, both positive and negative. When in low power role, it is often perceived to be too risky to offer negative feedback. Thus leaders don't hear the negatives and lose their ability to check reality and as a result feel immune to the consequences of abuse of power. Without feedback, leaders can be insulated from the feelings

associated with their impact, finding acting with empathy more difficult. In addition, leaders may become isolated and lonely leading to poorer judgment.

2. Our biologically inherent desire and capacity for empathy can easily be overridden by strong emotions such as anger, fear, and shame, because these strong emotions are responses to feeling threatened. When feeling danger our nervous systems revert from emotional intelligence to the less evolved nervous systems that are associated with fight, flight, or freeze.

3. We have all been wounded by misuses of power and there may be an unconscious tendency to treat others as we have been treated. Or we may in fact cause harm by overcompensating to avoid causing the same harm to others.

4. People can over-identify with their role power. They see their enhanced power as entirely personal rather than simply the authority of the role. This can lead to feelings of grandness and an unrealistic sense of self. When a leader has power associated with their role, they forget or override the kinds of respectful and beneficial behaviours that were effective before. When they see their role power simply as increased personal power, they can also begin misusing power in revenge for past hurt or maybe because now they can get away with it.

5. People often link role power with control, and as a result tend to become motivated by the fear of losing it, and sometimes too by the greed for more.

6. Many new leaders may feel insecure after being promoted to positions of authority, especially when they have had little

training or preparation. This insecurity tends to make them feel alone with negative emotions that go along with this.

7. Leaders can also become part of their organisational systems and cultures and it becomes difficult to act alone. These systems may well support or even mandate particular behaviours that contribute to right or wrong uses of power.

8. Most of the programmes and films we watch give rise to conditioned expectations about the use of power. We have become accustomed to thinking of power as manipulation, coercion and deception. We have come to understand that this is what power is and how it is effective. As a result we put up with this model of power and sanction it, even though it often causes harm.

So in putting the lessons of this book into practice, first of all ask yourself how important is being better at asking questions going to be for you in your work and personal level?

If on a scale of 1-10 you are up in the top quartile then start to think of what might be the first steps you can take. Choices you might have are:

- Think of some of the challenges you face at the moment

- Which questions might help you unlock some of the issues that you face

- What are your five favourite questions?

- How can you ask one new question a day?

- What questions are you good at asking right now and how could you make them even more powerful?

How Can I Start?

- How could you share some of these ideas with others?

- What about setting up an action learning group with others who have the same interest so that you can share experiences

- How good would it be (especially for me) to buy loads of copies of this book and send it out to all your friend and colleagues?

- Who do you work with where you have easy rapport already and where if you try these out even clunkily there won't be a problem?

- How about picking one new question a day and finding a way of using it during the day?

- What would you learn by more closely observing how others use questions are where they are missing opportunities

In Conclusion

Million Dollar Questions

From my experience I have found a number of questions super useful and I come back to them time and again. So if you have turned to the end of the book first you might wonder what you have missed. As well as being super-useful in coaching, negotiating, influencing, they will also work in this order:

1. What's the issue?

2. What makes it an issue NOW?

3. How important is it on a 1 - 10 scale?

4. How much energy do you have for a solution on a 1 - 10 scale?

5. Who owns this issue/problem?

6. In an ideal world what would be happening around this issue?

7. How would you know it had been resolved?

8. What's standing in the way of that ideal outcome?

9. What's going RIGHT here – even if it's only a bit?

10. Imagine you're at your most resourceful, what do you say to yourself about this issue?

11. What have you already tried?

12. What are the options for action here?

13. What criteria will you use to judge the options?

14. Which option seems the best one against those criteria?

15. So what's the next/first step?

16. When will you take it?

And finally some fun questions

- Why is the winner of Miss Universe always from Earth?
- Why is there only one Monopolies Commission?
- Why do some aircraft toilet windows have frosted glass?
- What was the best thing before sliced bread?
- How does a snowplough driver get to work in the morning?
- If you try to fail and succeed, what have you done?
- Why is there no other word for synonym?
- How much deeper would the sea be without sponges?
- Why do we nail down the lid of a coffin?
- If all generalisations are false, is this one?

The choice is of course and must be yours. Enjoy the journey!

Appendix - The Best Powerful Questions List

Top Ten Great Questions To Provide Focus

1. What would you rather have?

2. What do you want instead?

3. What will having this outcome do for me/us?

4. What are the downsides?

5. On a scale of 1-10 how important is this to you and what would get it to ten?

6. What might it feel like when you have achieved this outcome?

7. What other benefit are there?

8. What will success look like?

9. What would be a good outcome for ...?

10. What resources will you need to achieve this?

Top 10 Questions To Help You To Manage Emotions More Effectively

1. How are you feeling about this?

2. What is making you feel so strongly (passionately) about this?

3. I notice you feel strongly about this, tell me what that's about?

4. What needs to happen to resolve this?

5. How has …. led you to feel that way?

Appendix – The Best Powerful Questions List

6. What specifically are you feeling?

7. How do you think the other person is feeling about this?

8. How long have you felt this way?

9. On a scale of 1-10 how strongly do you feel about this?

10. What has triggered this feeling?

Top 5 Questions To Help You To Become More Self Aware

1. What were you thinking when you did that?

2. What would need to happen to be the best you, you could be

3. What's the story I'm telling myself here and how could I tell a more hopeful and empowering story about this same set of facts?

4. What if I'm wrong?

5. What will happen if you do change?

6. What will happen if you don't change?

7. What won't happen if you do change?

8. What won't happen if you don't change?

9. If you could make one change in your life, what would it be?

10. What would I do differently if I set out to win?

Top 10 Questions To Help You To Challenge Assumptions More Effectively

1. What assumptions are we making about this and how certain are we about them?

2. What would make a reasonable person act in this way

3. If you knew you are good enough, what would you do and how would you feel?

4. If you could make one change in your life, what would it be?

5. If you were not afraid, what would you do?

6. How confident are you about ... on a scale of 1-10? If not 10 what would get you to 10. If ten what are you assuming that gives you that belief?

7. If you knew the opposite to be true for you, what would you be doing, or what would be happening differently?

8. What would be a freeing assumption for you?

9. I am not sure I understand. Could you please explain it to me further?

10. What has led you to believe that?

Top 10 Questions To Help You To Challenge Assumptions More Effectively

1. What three things can you do **now** to reach your goals?

2. For each of these, what's smallest thing can you do today that will create momentum into tomorrow?

Appendix – The Best Powerful Questions List

3. What resistance do you expect to you idea, and how can you overcome it?

4. What are you willing to do to put your ideas into action?

5. List three reasons why someone would buy your idea, or product or service?

6. What tight deadlines can you give yourself?

7. What gives you the courage to act on your ideas?

8. Who could be part of your support system and how can you engage them?

9. What have you got or could you have at stake?

10. How could you burn your boats?

My Top 5 Questions To Help You To Become More Creative

1. What have you done differently today?

2. What if someone famous was trying to solve this problem

3. What would we do if we really tried to mess this up

4. What would happen if we had to double performance?

5. In what ways is implementing this project like starting a revolution?

Top 10 Questions To Help You To Promote Learning

1. What do you already know that might have relevance here?

2. What have we achieved so far?

3. What has helped or hindered progress?
4. What specifically was the difference that made the difference this time?
5. What have we learned from this experience and how will we use that knowledge?
6. How important is applying what you have learned in the future?
7. How have you made a difference today?
8. How has this experience helped in achieving our goal?
9. What do you notice when things are going well?
10. What do we need to do to get back on track?

Top 10 Questions To Help You To Promote Assertiveness

1. What makes you feel so strongly about this?
2. Could you tell me specifically how your proposal might work?
3. What are we trying to achieve here?
4. How is your proposal helping to achieve this outcome?
5. What other ways have you considered?
6. What might be the impact of this on…..?
7. How is behaving in this way helping here?
8. What do you need to resolve this?

Appendix – The Best Powerful Questions List

9. How can we work more effectively in the future?

10. What can I take more responsibility here?

Top 10 Questions To Help You To Promote Responsibility

1. What makes you feel so strongly about this?

2. Could you tell me specifically how your proposal might work?

3. What are we trying to achieve here?

4. How is your proposal helping to achieve this outcome?

5. What other ways have you considered?

6. What might be the impact of this on….?

7. How is behaving in this way helping here?

8. What do you need to resolve this?

9. How can we work more effectively in the future?

10. What can I take more responsibility here?

About The Author

Kevin Parker is a leading European consultant in the areas of change management, leadership and performance and is a qualified and experienced Executive Coach and Mediator.

He was, until 1994, the Senior Partner of PA Consulting Group's European Change Management Practice. Before this Kevin was HR Director at Lucas Service and Industrial Relations Manager in the Rover Group at Longbridge. He is an honours graduate in Economics from the University of Bristol. He has been entered in the 'Who's Who' of Britain's Business Elite. He is a qualified Executive coach, NLP practitioner, Mediator and an alumnus of the Wharton Executive Programme.

He is joint author of several books: 'How to Take Part In The Quality Revolution', 'The Total Quality Experience', Sailing Through Six Sigma' and 'Management Consulting'. He has also led in the past research to enhance consulting services in major change, visiting a wide range of world--- class companies in Japan, the USA, and Europe. He maintains strong links with Wharton Business School (USA) and Erasmus Business School in Holland on areas of Strategy and Leadership.

Kevin has been guiding many clients in maximising the potential of their organisations through strategically focussed leadership and change programmes, since the mid 80's. The wide range of his clients include:

British Telecom, Midlands Electricity, Scottish Power and Scottish Water **Paper industry:** UPM Kymmene, James River, Amcor, and Tullis Russell, Cosworth Engineering, Polaroid, Ulster Weavers, Kohler, ABB, Grontmij, National Semiconductor, Agusta Westland, and OKI, Rémy

About The Author

Cointreau; Weetabix, ING Bank, RBS, and Zurich Insurance, J Sainsbury and M&S, Orange, BBC, Exact Software, Reid Publishing, Ocean Group, BA, Nidera, NWDA, Highland and Islands Enterprise, UK Sport, Strathclyde University, DWP, Foreign & Commonwealth Office, Football Foundation, Scottish Enterprise

Kevin has maintained long term relationships with senior managers in many of these organisations. They value 1:1 coaching sessions with him, to help explore their future outcomes and develop their confidence for the future.

As a certified practitioner and trainer of NLP, one of Kevin's key attributes is also his ability to assist individuals and teams in realising their potential, through an understanding of how top achievers think and act on a habitual basis.

He is a qualified RYA Yacht Master and often organises events on sailing yachts for leadership and team development

Kevin is a great coach and trainer in the field of leadership. It is always a pleasure and also insightful to work with him. Recent quote from one of my clients: "we want more Kevin!' - Martijn Rademakers Director, Centre for Strategy & Leadership

Kevin is one of the best leadership experts I know, whose energetic and social style always gets everyone in a group involved. Probably his biggest strength is that he makes leadership tangible and practical, helping managers to translate theory into practice.' - Ron Meyer, Managing Director, CSL

Kevin offers top-drawer senior management experience in the form of leadership delivery, executive coaching, and strategy. Having worked with Kevin on joint projects, I highly recommend Kevin and all that he can offer in this field. Charasmatic, intelligent and a very loyal person. - Gilly Salter, MD GSA Consulting,

Kevin has worked with Linac on several occasions and I feel that I can very strongly endorse his work. Its been a pleasure to work with Kevin he has always been totally responsive and focused. Kevin has substantial experience and this depth and breadth of experience coupled with exceptional subject knowledge always manifests itself in first class creative solutions and excellent client feedback. I would strongly recommend Kevin to any organisation. Andrew Terry, *MD Linac,*

'Kevin is a dynamic, active consultant who is always open to new ideas and learning new approaches. His boundless energy means that he works hard and fast, turning jobs round far more quickly than many other excellent colleagues. In addition he is easy to work with and ready to take on board other people's ideas. I always enjoy working with Kevin; he is straightforward, down to earth and, perhaps unusually, brings a strong balance of business acumen, commercial knowledge and attention to people. Matt Driver, *Management, Consultant, Trainer, Coach and Author*

Kevin was a long-standing and respected associate of Management Futures when I was CEO there in 2006/7. I had personal experience of his performance in a leadership development programme and in winning an important executive coaching assignment for a major UK mobile telephone operator. - Charles McLachlan

I worked together with Kevin for almost 2 years as a coach and trainer in international leadership programs. Working together with him is fun and I enjoy his professionalism in change management and coaching. I have learned a lot from him and he is an inspiring person. His interest is providing the best service for the customer. He surprises colleagues and customers with new ideas and approaches. Hiring Kevin for a training or as a personal coach is an excellent and no risk investment. Bernadette Kester, HR Director Nidera

About The Author

Kevin is a first class coach and mentor. His understanding of people and therefore leadership is in my experience is unrivalled. His expertise crosses across many fields in the strategic and operational aspects of business. I am pleased to add that personally Kevin has made a significant difference in certain aspects of my approach to business, which has also improved my career path.' **Top qualities:** *Great Results, Expert, High Integrity - Phil Davis Interim HR Director*

Kevin is a real 'people person' - unflappable and easy-going in all his dealings. He has a knack for bringing people out and always seems to know how to deal with situations that may (and do) arise. He is a non-competitive and quietly confrontational - vital attribute in the environments in which he works. He is also a kind and thoughtful man. Margaret Dewhurst, Director, Boardroom Associates Ltd

I have known and worked with Kevin for some 12 years. Kevin is an exceptional senior executive coach and facilitator with the ability to inspire board level and senior managers to think well beyond their normal scope in both a personal and business context. He is much praised by clients when facilitating and coaching in extremely difficult situations David Coates,

Bibliography

Beaver, D., *Easy Being* (Useful Book Co. 1997)

Blanchard, K. H., Zigarmi. P. & D., *Leadership & The One Minute Manager* (HarperCollins Business 2000)

Covey, S. R., *Seven Habits Of Highly Effective People* (Simon & Schuster 2004)

Dickson, A., *Difficult Conversations* (Piatkus Books 2006)

Driver, M., *Coaching Positively* (Open University Press 2011)

Dweck, C., *Mindset* (Robinson 2007)

Fisher, R., Ury, W., Patto, B., *Getting To Yes* (Random House Business Books 1997)

Gallwey, T., The Inner Game Of Work: Overcoming Mental Obstacles For Maximum Performance (Texere Publishing 1997)

Goffee, R. and Jones, G., *Why Would Anyone Want To Be Led By You?* (Harvard Business School Press 2006)

Goleman, D., Emotional Intelligence: Why It Can Matter More Than IQ (Bloomsbury 1996)

Hickman, C., Smith, T., Connors, R., *The Oz Principle* (Portfolio 1998)

Kline, N., Time to Think: Listening to Ignite the Human Mind (Cassell Illustrated 2002)

Patterson, K., Grenny, J., McMillan, R., and Switzler, A., *Crucial Confrontations* (McGraw-Hill Professional 2004)

Rock, D., *Your Brain At Work* (Harper Collins 2009)

Rosenberg, M. B., and Gandhi, A., *Non Violent Communication* (Puddledancer Press 2003)

Seligman, Martin E.P., *Authentic Happiness* (Nicholas Brealey Publishing Ltd 2003)

Stewart, I and Joines, V., *T A Today: A New Introduction to Transactional Analysis* (Lifespace Publishing, Revised 2012)

Stone, Patton, & Heen, *Difficult Conversations* (Penguin Books 2000)

Whitmore, Sir John., Coaching For Performance: Growing People, Performance And Purpose, (Nicholas Brealey Publishing 2002)

Lightning Source UK Ltd.
Milton Keynes UK
UKOW06f1218200314

228460UK00001B/1/P

9 781910 162736